Does Redistricting Make a Difference?

Does Redistricting Make a Difference?

Partisan Representation
and Electoral Behavior

MARK E. RUSH

THE JOHNS HOPKINS UNIVERSITY PRESS

Baltimore and London

© 1993 The Johns Hopkins University Press
All rights reserved
Printed in the United States of American on acid-free paper

The Johns Hopkins University Press
2715 North Charles Street
Baltimore, Maryland 21218-4139
The Johns Hopkins Press Ltd., London

Library of Congress Cataloging-in-Publication Data

Rush, Mark E.
    Does redistricting make a difference? : partisan representation
and electoral behavior / Mark E. Rush.
       p.   cm.
    Includes bibliographical references and index.
    ISBN 0-8018-4579-3 (alk. paper)
    1. Gerrymander.   2. Apportionment (Electoral law)—United States.
3. Election districts—United States.   4. Voting—United States.
5. Representative government and representation—United States.
I. Title.
JK1347.R87   1993
328.73'07345—dc20   93-6670

A catalog record for this book is available from the British Library.

For Flor and William

Contents

Preface and Acknowledgments

This work is a skeptical inquiry into the gerrymandering controversy and a critical assessment of the theoretical assumptions that underpin prevailing legal and political analyses of the redistricting process. Gerrymandering engenders controversy because it is regarded as a means of denying fair representational opportunity to political groups. Such an argument makes sense, however, only if certain questionable assumptions about individual and group voting behavior hold true and if a significant part of the study of voting behavior is ignored.

Of course, there are different types of gerrymandering and different methods of repairing their damage. This work focuses specifically on partisan gerrymandering as distinct from racial gerrymandering. This differentiation is a key premise of the book: racial gerrymandering is much easier to perpetrate, detect, and remedy than partisan gerrymandering. As a result, the two must be studied, analyzed, and remedied differently. I argue that partisan gerrymandering, qua the denial of representational opportunity to a particular group of partisans, is in fact virtually impossible to prove; furthermore, its impact is unsubstantiated by political science research.

What I found striking when I first embarked upon this research was the failure in many circles to acknowledge that different political groups may behave differently and therefore need to be studied differently. Reading through Supreme Court decisions concerning redistricting and commentaries thereon, one can come to believe that, as far as representation and voting behavior are concerned, groups are groups, period. Black voters, Republicans, men, women, the 4-H Club, the League of Women Voters—they are all political groups with idiosyncratic interests that are held dear by their respective members. Furthermore, it is generally assumed that group members will behave as conscious dedicated partisans and therefore will vote and ally themselves in predictably partisan, group-oriented patterns. Although this sounds reasonable or even self-evident, it is simply not always the case. Dissenting in *Davis v. Bandemer,* Justice Sandra Day O'Connor acknowledged this when she pointed out that different political groups behave differently. Whereas racial group membership is immutable, partisan group membership is not. Accordingly, the two could not be represented—or denied their fair representational opportunity as a result of a gerrymander—in the same way.

Prior to this statement by Justice O'Connor, little had been said to this effect by the Court or by its observers in either the legal or political science community. Research and criticism of the Court's decisions in the area of voting rights and representation have either ignored or simply felt no compulsion to address the difference between partisan and racial groups. As a result, the research and theories developed about representational fairness, political group behavior, and the impact of gerrymandering have been constructed in part on false, or at least untested, propositions.

Accordingly, this work is not merely a study of a political phenomenon; it is as well a commentary on the role of political science in analyzing such phenomena. Political science plays an important role in shaping the way in which people think about politics. By casting gerrymandering as a method of harming groups of voters without first elaborating on the differences among groups, political science has exacerbated the controversy surrounding the issue. I hope this book will help clarify some of the vagaries of the methods of redistricting analysis employed currently by political and legal scholars and thereby alleviate some of the tension that surrounds the gerrymandering issue.

Although many people deserve thanks for their patience and generosity in supporting and commenting upon this research, several are especially deserving. David Petersen, my research assistant at Washington and Lee University, performed yeoman service in helping to prepare the final version of this manuscript. I thank my dissertation advisers, Richard Katz and Milton Cummings, for their patience and guidance in developing the core thesis. I am grateful as well to Bernie Grofman and Arend Lijphart for their kindness and generosity in giving inciteful criticisms and commentary at critical times in the development of this work. Finally, I cannot begin to thank enough or describe adequately the role played by Woody Howard, Jr., in helping to make this a better piece of research. His generous comments and thoughtful criticism improved immeasurably the quality of this work. He is certainly the greatest mentor with whom I have had the privilege to study. I hope that in my lifetime I will inspire my students as much as he inspired me in a single class.

Does Redistricting Make a Difference?

Introduction: Defining the Gerrymander

If politics makes strange bedfellows, then the American redistricting process has become a national political orgy of bacchanalian proportions. Few other aspects of American political life so regularly enlist the participation and interest of such a multitude of players from all parts of the political spectrum. The roster of participants in this decennial political revel reads like the annual index to the *Congressional Quarterly* or the *National Journal,* and it includes everyone from Supreme Court justices to political consultants and state legislators.

Party organizations, incumbent legislators, and myriad interest groups partake in the process of redrawing state legislative and congressional district lines with an intensity that reflects their fervent belief that their political fortunes are at stake. They spend millions of dollars in campaign contributions to hire political consultants and technicians who, they hope, will be able to maximize the benefits or minimize the damages to their party when district lines are finally settled.[1] State legislatures themselves (especially those whose congressional delegations are losing seats) become involved in the redistricting process, since the constitution entrusts the states with the responsibility of equitably redrawing district lines. The discretionary power that state legislators wield is so immense that the national parties actually coach their members in Congress on how to cultivate and maintain good relations with their respective state governments. Nervous congressional incumbents frequently return home from Washington to plead for the preservation of their most favored constituencies.[2]

Ultimately, the federal and state courts are responsible for deciding which maps are fair—and therefore constitutional—and which are not. While the Supreme Court serves as final referee, the various lower federal courts serve as battlegrounds for political groups who contend that they have been disadvantaged by redistricting schemes that dilute their influence by splitting their members into two or more districts. These groups assert, and the Supreme Court has thus far agreed, that such vote dilution denies the afflicted group its fair opportunity to be represented and is therefore unconstitutional because it violates the Fourteenth Amendment's equal protection clause.

The Supreme Court's job has been to decide when such gerrymandering claims are indeed valid. However, it has been hampered by the inability to set forth an enduring standard with which it can identify a gerrymander. This obstacle has arisen—and has become increasingly insurmountable—for two reasons. First, the increasing sophistication of computer technology now permits mapmakers to devise virtually infinite numbers of redistricting plans that can undermine even the most stringent criteria for fair districting.[3] Second, and perhaps more important, the concept of gerrymandering—along with assumptions about voting behavior, partisan loyalty, and representation upon which it is based—has yet to be defined with any clarity or consistency. The term *gerrymander* was first used in 1812 when the Democrat-Republican (i.e., Jeffersonian) majority of the Massachusetts legislature split Essex County in order to dilute the strength of the Federalists. A local newspaper described the shape of the new district as a "gerrymander" in honor of Governor Elbridge Gerry, who approved the new districting plan, and because it resembled the outline of the mythical salamander.[4]

Although the term originally described only the form of a legislative boundary, its modern meaning is much more complex and less specific. It was originally a pejorative term because, the strange shape of the district notwithstanding, it referred to creative cartography intended to prevent a candidate from being reelected. Ironically, this first gerrymander backfired: in the next year's elections, the Federalists recaptured the district even though it was full of voters who, it seemed, would not support them.[5]

This short, sordid episode of American history raises the questions: Where was the injustice in this gerrymander? Who was injured? Who was to blame? These questions are key to an understanding of gerrymandering in the current political context because, in the wake of Supreme Court decisions such as *Baker v. Carr* and *Reynolds v. Sims,* the meaning of the term *gerrymander* has taken many forms, all of which are predicated on the belief that someone, somewhere, has been injured as a result of the redrawing of legislative district lines. In order to determine who exactly the injured parties are, we must first clarify the difference between *gerrymandering* and a benign form of altering constituency boundary lines, *redistricting.* The latter is easier to define: redistricting is the process whereby legislative districts are redrawn, usually to equalize the population of each district. Gerrymandering is a more problematic concept because definitions are frequently unclear regarding (1) who the injured parties are, (2) what it means to be represented, and (3) what it means to be denied a fair opportunity to be represented. This is not to say that definitions are in short supply; a short survey of some of the more recent attempts to define the term indicates that the concept's breadth and complexity make it more like a chameleon than a salamander.

In "Considering the Gerrymander," for example, Leroy Hardy surveys several encyclopedias and dictionaries in order to find a common thread among the various definitions of *gerrymander* (245). He concludes that "gerrymandering is a technique used for partisan purpose in the creation of constituencies . . . [which entails] the consolidation of opposition strength" in an "arbitrary" or "unnatural" manner (247). Such a definition is incomplete, however, because it implies that there are acceptable natural or nonarbitrary means of drawing district lines yet he fails to explain what they are. Although Hardy goes on to discuss "what a gerrymander is not" (264), he never explains clearly how to distinguish a gerrymander from a nongerrymander.

No clear interpretation of *gerrymander* has yet been set forth; definitions proffered thus far invariably address only bits and pieces of the concept. Gerrymandering is more than malicious political cartography; its evils go beyond the inconvenience to incumbents of trying to convert voters in newly drawn constituencies; it involves more than the rights of legislative minority parties to block redistricting actions by majority cartographers. In order to substantiate the claims of foul play that justify the political controversy characterizing the redistricting process, the sine qua non of any accurate definition of gerrymandering is the alteration of district lines in order to deny or impair the representational opportunity of a group of voters who, under other circumstances (i.e., a different districting plan), could, if they so desired, coalesce to ensure the election of a candidate who would serve as their delegate to a legislative assembly. Representational denial implies that voters—not individual legislators—are the principal victims of gerrymanders. Although it may smack of unfairness, the dismissal of individual incumbents is problematic in this context only insofar as it can be argued that their demise results directly in the diminished representation of a particular political group. The purpose of this book is to develop and analyze this core definition by studying the assumptions that underlie it in order to determine whether or not gerrymandering and the possibility of representational denial actually exist and whether or not the definition and underlying assumptions are supported by empirical evidence.

Of course, in a single-member plurality district system of representation (SMP) such as that used in the United States, some groups of voters are always denied representation because of the system's winner-take-all method of vote counting. In any given district, there are always two groups of voters: the overrepresented winners and the underrepresented losers. Accordingly, in an SMP system, the *opportunity to be represented* is for all intents and purposes the *opportunity to vote with a group of like-minded voters large enough to be a majority in a given district*. When, therefore, does *losing* become tantamount to *denial* of representational opportunity?

In order to answer this question we must first decide who is being represented—who, that is, are the constituent groups? In general, gerrymandering analysts refer to two particular types of groups: racial groups and partisan groups (that is, the parties-in-the-electorate). Thus individual candidates, particular towns, or local clusters of voters are not, in and of themselves, prey for gerrymanders. They are prey only insofar as they are members of larger partisan or racial groups who, if district lines are drawn in nonarbitrary or natural manners, will be capable of voting as a majority in some of the legislative districts. If Republicans are a majority of the voters in city X, which, by itself, is large enough to comprise a legislative district, the division of the city in a way that prevents the Republicans from being a majority in any district would be regarded as a gerrymander.[6] If, on the other hand, Republicans (or any other plaintiff group) are so few in number or are spread so thinly across a state that no natural or nonarbitrary districting scheme could afford them the possibility to coalesce and act as a local majority, they could not be said to be gerrymanderable.

Current definitions of gerrymandering harp on the evil that it inflicts upon group representation. Gerrymanderers are said to achieve their partisan goals by lessening the likelihood that concentrations of partisans will be able to act as local majorities so that a statewide majority of the same partisans will be able to elect a majority of legislators. These definitions are compromised, however, by the fact that SMP systems naturally treat local majorities and minorities unfairly.

Much of the defining and redefining of gerrymandering has occurred in or in reaction to Supreme Court decisions. Writing in 1967, Robert Dixon contends that gerrymandering is simply "discriminatory districting. . . . It equally covers squiggles, multimember districting, or simple nonaction, when the result is racial or political malrepresentation."[7] The Court has expanded upon the idea of "malrepresentation" by asserting that "each political group in a State should have the same chance to elect representatives of its choice as any other political group" (*Davis v. Bandemer,* 124). Confusion arises when analysts seek to define exactly what they mean by "malrepresentation" or impaired chances to elect representatives.

On more than one occasion, the Court has contended that the unconstitutional aspect of gerrymandering is a function of *conscious* attempts to lessen the impact of one group's votes. Hence, Justices Abe Fortas and Lewis Powell defined gerrymandering as "the deliberate and arbitrary distortion of district boundaries and populations for partisan or personal political purposes."[8] But these political purposes must be discriminatory; as Justice Byron White noted, someone must be injured in order to claim that they have been gerrymandered: "Unconstitutional discrimination occurs only when the electoral system is arranged in a manner that will consistently degrade a voter's or group of voters' influence on the political process as a whole" (*Davis,* 139). If, on the other hand, all concerned parties agree to a given districting plan, the observation that the plan nonetheless discriminates against certain voting groups is irrelevant.[9]

Although malicious intent is a component of a gerrymander, the justices have disagreed regarding its necessity as a basis for a gerrymandering claim. In *Rogers v. Lodge,* the Court contended that a racial gerrymander did not necessarily need to be expressly intentional.[10] Instead, it held that prima facie evidence of discriminatory impact would suffice as a basis upon which to substantiate a vote dilution claim. Four years later, the Court reasserted this with regard to partisan gerrymandering. Regardless of the motivations of the legislators who drew the district lines, *results* are the key component of an unconstitutional gerrymander: "Even if a state legislature redistricts with the specific intention of disadvantaging one political party's election prospects, we do not believe that there has been an unconstitutional discrimination against members of that party unless the redistricting does in fact disadvantage it at the polls" (*Davis,* 139). Ironically, these criteria suggest that the original gerrymander in Massachusetts would not necessarily be regarded as a gerrymander today. Since the Federalists recaptured the district despite the Jeffersonians' intentions, it would be difficult to argue that the former had been disadvantaged at the polls.

Electoral disadvantage in an SMP electoral system is thus more than simply losing a district election; it is the relegation of a group to minority status despite the fact that, under other circumstances, it would not be so condemned. This raises the question, Was the 1812 redistricting a "temporary" gerrymander? When the districts were first drawn, the Federalists seemed condemned to minority status; nonetheless, they won back the district. What happened? Clearly, their opportunity to be represented or elect legislators of their choice was not completely destroyed. Unless we assume that all of the Federalists who had been cut out of the district moved into that part of Essex County that was still in the district, we must infer that the Federalist candidate attracted voters across party lines. Since the Jeffersonians' intentions would not necessarily be relevant for deeming the redistricting plan to be a gerrymander, and the results of this clearly *political* manipulation of district lines obviously backfired, we can conclude that the 1812 gerrymander was not a gerrymander. What then is a gerrymander in the modern context?

The contention that a gerrymander results in the actual denial or impairment of a group's representational opportunity presupposes the existence of durable, identifiable groups of voters. But not all groups are so durable or identifiable. Racial groups and their representational opportunity are easily discernible: we can account for their size and geographic dispersion simply by counting individuals. The identification of partisan groups (Democrats- and Republicans-in-the-electorate) and their representational opportunity presents a difficult empirical problem, because their members are not so easily counted. The standards for identifying voters as Democrat or Republican are varied. One may be a candidate bearing a party's label, a card-carrying, dues-paying member of a party, a citizen registered as a party member, or a voter—registered affiliation notwithstanding—who casts a vote for a party's candidate in a given election. Any one of these qualifications can be used to identify a citizen as a member of one party or the other. Yet, since the qualifications are not mutually exclusive, one can be a Democrat by one measure and a Republican by another.

Furthermore, representational opportunity (and, therefore, its denial or impairment) is different for racial and partisan groups. A black leader might assert that, in his racially torn area, all voting blacks vote Democratic; his claim can be substantiated by voting returns from his district.[11] A similar claim about

Republican voters, however, can be supported or refuted by reference to any of the qualifications cited above. Registration data may indicate that a district is heavily Republican, but election results may suggest otherwise. Also, a given "Republican" district might vote Republican only at some electoral levels, while supporting Democratic candidates at others. Although the assurance of representational opportunity might be rather easy to enforce in racially polarized areas, assuring partisan representational opportunity is much more difficult. Though candidates run under party labels, election data indicate that voters who affiliate with a party do not always vote for that party's candidate. How then are such voters to be regarded—by their professed partisanship or by their voting behavior?

This volume focuses on specifically partisan gerrymandering, because the groups of voters involved in such partisan disputes are much more difficult to identify, measure, or define than those of racial gerrymandering cases. Racial-gerrymandering analysis is easier to undertake, because the groups involved exist and can be identified independent of their behavior at the polls. Because partisan groups can be said to exist only as a function of expressed political loyalties or electoral behavior, partisan-gerrymandering analysis cannot operate on the same assumptions that underlie racial-gerrymandering analysis. Thus the former requires that we account for the fact that the targets of gerrymandering—the parties-in-the electorate—are constantly changing their size, membership, and cohesion, whereas racial groups are, on all three counts, much more consistent over time.

Electoral studies indicate that consistent and coherent individual voting patterns are not necessarily the rule. Thus, what appears to be a cohesive group of partisans in one election might not appear as such in the next.[12] Those who seek to define gerrymandering have consistently overlooked this point. For the purposes of redistricting analysis, *group* is obviously a very fuzzy term. In some cases, blacks and whites may vote as cohesive blocs; in others, blacks may be concentrated into a densely populated geographic area (and therefore be easily identifiable) but may not vote with any degree of partisan cohesion.[13] Finally, some groups may feel a strong sense of ethnic or religious cohesion yet, due to other demographic factors, not be recognized as such by lawmakers.[14]

The difficulty in addressing partisan-gerrymandering claims lies in the fact that party labels such as "Democrat" can refer to the elites that compose the party-in-the-government or to the mass party-in-the-electorate. When legislators redistrict, they often seek to reorganize the party-in-the-electorate in order to adjust the strength of the party-in-the-government. But, since the party-in-the-electorate is much less organized and cohesive than the party-in-the-government, we cannot expect the former to act as a partisan monolith when redistricted. A partisan-gerrymander claim therefore requires a showing that the representational opportunity of partisan voters has been denied or impaired as a result of the redrawing of district lines. This is no easy task, because the partisan preferences of voters, unlike their race, are not necessarily fixed.

Voters may change the way they vote, as Massachusetts voters did in 1812 after new district boundary lines had been drawn.

If voters are at all likely to change their partisan behavior, then they cannot be said to have been denied the opportunity to be represented simply because in a given year they surge to vote for the candidates of one party and, therefore, appear to be underrepresented. They can just as easily surge toward the other party in the next election. Fluidity of partisan preference complicates the identification of partisan electoral division within a constituency, because the number of party voters (and, therefore, the size of the party-in-the-electorate) will not be constant. This is not to say that voting is a strictly random act. Nevertheless, this fluidity prevents gerrymandering analysts from making references to political groups without first explaining their basis for grouping voters who do not behave consistently as group members.

This variability of partisan electoral behavior has been overlooked by the overwhelming majority of representation theorists and redistricting analysts. By analysts, I refer here to the judiciary—especially the Supreme Court—as well as to political scientists. Over the last three decades, the courts have been the principal laboratory of redistricting analysis and debate. For the most part, political science has played a secondary or passive role, either as a resource upon which courts and litigants rely for evidence or as a source of post hoc analysis of the impact of judicial decisions. Both the courts and political science have approached problems of redistricting and partisan gerrymandering from a perspective founded upon questionable assumptions about voting behavior, political partisanship, and representation. As a result, the courts have encountered many doctrinal and conceptual problems in their attempts to create a coherent body of redistricting law grounded in constitutional principles. Political science, on the other hand, has produced analyses in which empirical evidence conflicts with or even contradicts prevailing normative beliefs about voting and representation.

The key source of confusion in the resolution of redistricting controversies is the absence of a coherent, generally accepted definition of fair representation and the lack of a consensus concerning the role and functions of electoral systems. In addition, no constitutional standard exists by which the courts can measure the inherent fairness of the single-member plurality electoral system. The absence of a constitutional definition of *fair representation* or *political group* comes as no surprise, since the fear of faction and a general distaste for parties pervaded the ranks of the Federalists and Anti-Federalists alike.[15] Madison's government of divided federal powers was designed not only to prevent factions from taking over the entire government but also to manufacture broad governing coalitions at the expense of discrete or local interests. Nonetheless, some observers now contend that the Supreme Court is destined to find the single-member plurality system of voting unconstitutional and that, in time, some form of proportional representation will be instituted to replace it.[16]

The constitutional fairness of the SMP system is actually a moot question, since electoral systems are merely embodiments of decision rules for the counting of votes. They may discriminate against certain types of groups (for example, groups that are small or whose constituents are dispersed), but a system in and of itself is not inherently biased against groups with particular ideologies.[17] In addition, the propriety of an inquiry into the constitutional fairness of the SMP system seems questionable. Not all electoral systems are designed to ensure that every political tendency in a society is represented in proportion to its strength. In fact, one of the strengths of the SMP system is the fact that it encourages the formation of a legislative majority; it thus forces the building of coalitions and militates against the proliferation of small parties and factionalism.

Since the Constitution is silent regarding electoral systems, the Court has had to fashion its own definitions of political group and representational fairness. As a result, it has come under heavy fire for addressing the political questions inherent in redistricting analysis, since it has no constitutional standard upon which to base its decisions. One of the earliest and most vocal criticisms was expressed by Justice Felix Frankfurter in *Colegrove v. Green,* and later in *Baker v. Carr:*

> Talk of "debasement" or "dilution" is circular talk. One cannot speak of "debasement" or "dilution" of the value of a vote until there is first defined a standard of reference as to what a vote should be worth. What is actually asked of the Court in this case is to choose among competing bases of representation—ultimately, really, among competing theories of political philosophy—in order to establish an appropriate frame of government for the state of Tennessee and thereby for all the States in the Union. (*Baker,* 300, Frankfurter, J., dissenting)

Whether the Supreme Court should have entered the political thicket of reapportionment and redistricting is now a moot question, since the Court has been deciding cases in this area for the better part of three decades. This work focuses on the approach taken by the courts and political scientists in analyzing three issues: the concept and definition of representation, the definition of *political group* and the measurement of its fair representational opportunity, and the political science assumptions about voting behavior and political partisanship on which the Court's decisions have been based.

The Court's original task in reapportionment cases was merely to decide whether the populations of legislative and congressional districts in given states must be equal in order to ensure that voters in different districts could have equal impact on the legislative process.[18] However, its involvement with questions of group representation and fair representational opportunity in gerrymandering cases unearthed empirical problems that expose the weakness of its assumptions about voting behavior and partisanship. Traditional analysis of redistricting decisions has been predicated upon a number of underlying beliefs:

1. Partisan behavior is consistent from election to election.
2. Therefore, voters can be easily classified as group members who tend to vote for their group's candidate most of the time.
3. Therefore, the size of political groups is easily determined by referring to election results.
4. Therefore, the fair representation of groups as well as the denial of fair representational opportunity can be determined simply by comparing the percentage of the vote received by a given group and its percentage of seats in a given legislative body.
5. Finally, it is presumed that votes cast for one party in one district have the same meaning as votes cast for the same party in another district—regardless of who the candidates are.

The analysis of voting behavior in Massachusetts and Connecticut undermines the assumption of consistent partisan behavior and thereby strikes at a fundamental assumption of representation theories: that partisan constituencies—voting blocs—can be identified clearly, accurately, and easily. In addition, representation theory, as well as judicial and political science analyses, presupposes that electoral groups are consistent in their size and behavior; my findings suggest that this is not the case because voters frequently join and quit political parties. Accordingly, we cannot ascertain or define a voter's partisanship if that voter's loyalties shift back and forth between the parties. For the same reason, we cannot ascertain such a voter's group membership or, therefore, measure the size of the group to which we say the voter belongs, because other voters are also likely to shift back and forth as well. Thus, variable partisan behavior produces variable group size, which, in turn, militates against efforts to determine a group's fair representation or its fair representational opportunity.

Recent analyses have already begun to criticize the Supreme Court's approach to voting rights and minority vote dilution cases because the Court seems unable to decide what it means by fair representational opportunity.[19] If we cannot decide what fair representational opportunity is in racial gerrymandering cases, where the conflicting groups are clearly defined, then we are even less able to do so in partisan gerrymandering cases, where the size and nature of the conflicting groups (the political-parties-in-the-electorate) are in a state of flux. Although the Court has never contended that political parties are entitled to the same special constitutional protections that racial minorities receive, the Court's opinions have expressed a belief that partisan groups are as easily identifiable as racial groups. Although skin color offers a clear indication of racial group membership, measures of partisan electoral behavior do not necessarily indicate partisan group membership. An assessment of the validity of this belief serves as the starting point for this analysis.

The Court's Approach to Gerrymandering and Representation

When discussing the role of the Supreme Court in American politics, it is sometimes instructive to address what it does not or is supposed not to do. The Court is, for example, a reactive body that for the most part can hear cases only on appeal from lower courts. It therefore is not empowered to initiate inquiries or offer advisory opinions on policy matters pending before other branches of the government.[1]

Another way of viewing the Court is from the perspective of what it is capable of doing. In this sense, we do not seek to discuss the nature of the powers bestowed upon it by the Constitution; instead, we address questions of the Court's capacity to use these powers and the limits of their effectiveness. The litigatory process, by nature piecemeal and incremental, lends itself well to the narrowing down of broad principles of federalism and the interpretation of concepts such as freedom of expression. However, this process is ill-suited for resolving policy-oriented issues or clarifying concepts that are not especially well-defined.[2]

The concept of fair representation in a single-member plurality system of elections is a good example of an issue whose resolution does not lend itself to the litigatory process. An SMP electoral system, by definition, is not designed to produce mathematically fair election results. Instead, its design ensures that the party that wins the most votes will tend to be overrepresented. As a result, the Court's efforts to build a case law of representation have been stymied with each attempt to apply a conception of fairness grounded in the principle of equal protection to a system of elections whose design and function fly in the face of such an idea.

The Court's propounding of the idea that political groups are entitled to equal representational opportunity—despite the inequalities inherent in SMP voting systems—has been further troubled by its inability to define clearly its concept of a political group. Its principal contention has been that all politically relevant groups are entitled to participate in the electoral process and to do so with equal opportunities to win legislative seats. Such a definition begs further clarification of the term *relevant*. Whereas the Court's dicta make it clear that blondes, bicyclists, and boy scouts do not meet its criteria for politically relevant groups, its decisions do not indicate why some groups (such as racial groups) count and others (such as ethnic groups) do not. Hence, in *United Jewish Organizations of Williamsburg v. Carey*, the Court tolerated the denial of representational opportunity to Hasidic Jews in order to enhance the opportunity of blacks. In fairness to the Court, it should be noted that this case involved a statutory interpretation of Section 5 of the Voting Rights Act. The statute designated which groups were to be protected; Hasidics were not on the list, blacks were. Nonetheless, the theoretical problem of establishing a clear and consistent measure for deciding which groups count as politically relevant endures.

The Court's other difficulty has been to decide what it means by fair representational opportunity. On several occasions the Court has taken pains to assert that the SMP system is not unconstitutional; in addition it has remained unreceptive to calls for the establishment of a system of proportional representation. Furthermore, the actual size of the groups in question has not always been easily determined. Thus, the Court set before itself the Sisyphean task of establishing principles by which groups of indeterminate size could be assured of their fair representational opportunity in a system of elections designed to militate against proportionally fair electoral outcomes. The result of this venture has been the creation of a case law of representation that is laden with unclear terminology, confused concepts, and conflicting precedents, as well as incorrect assumptions about voting behavior, political partisanship, and representation. The task that the Court set for itself requires means beyond the scope of its power.

The Current Setting: *Davis v. Bandemer*

In *Davis v. Bandemer* (1986), the Supreme Court ruled that partisan gerrymanders were justiciable. In so doing, the Court brought itself to the edge of a "second reapportionment revolution."[3] The first revolution erupted in the early 1960s, when the Court first chose to hear reapportionment cases, previously avoided because they involved political questions.[4] This decision constituted a significant change in the Court's behavior, opening new avenues of adjudication and case law. The *Davis* decision was similarly earthshaking because previously the Court had heard only those redistricting complaints filed by ethnic groups. Despite the Court's rejection of the Democratic plaintiffs' claim that the redistricting of the Indiana legislature was unconstitutional, Justice White, speaking for the plurality, took pains to assert that political groups were as entitled to equal protection as any other group that made a claim of discrimination (*Davis*, 125). Justice White rejected the argument that the Court should avoid such questions of partisan gerrymandering, despite their inherently political nature,[5] because "disposition of [such questions] does not involve [the

Court] in a matter more properly decided by a coequal branch of our Government . . . [nor is this Court] persuaded that there are no judicially discernible and manageable standards by which political gerrymander cases are to be decided" (*Davis*, 123).

The Court was sharply divided on the issue. In her dissent, Justice Sandra Day O'Connor, joined by Chief Justice Warren Burger and Justice William Rehnquist, questioned the nature of the groups to which any judicial standard, regardless of its manageability, might be applied. She maintained that there was a great difference between racial groups and political parties. Membership in the former, she stated, "is an immutable characteristics," while "voters can— and often do—move from one party to the other or support candidates from both parties." Accordingly, "vote dilution analysis is far less manageable when extended to major political parties than if confined to racial minority groups" (*Davis*, 156). Thus, while the majority asserted that the Court *did* have the capacity to fashion a usable, consistent standard by which claims of vote dilution could be measured, the minority maintained that some groups lack sufficient cohesiveness or behavioral consistency to be measurable, regardless of the quality or the theoretical soundness of the fairness measure.

This divergence among the justices was not due simply to a disagreement regarding the facts of the *Davis* case. The justices addressed two distinctly different, albeit related, questions. Those who asserted the manageability of a judicial measure of gerrymandering did not address its applicability to a heterogeneous and fragmented electorate. The three dissenters focused instead on the volatility of electoral behavior. They concluded—questions of representational fairness notwithstanding—that even if such a manageable standard could be deduced, the Court could not apply it to a society composed of groups that vary in their cohesiveness. The difference of opinion among the justices is the predictable result of the Court's failure first to investigate and then to establish coherent models of (1) individual and group rights to vote and to be represented, (2) actual voting behavior, and (3) partisanship. Furthermore, the Court has not considered carefully the diverse definitions of the term *representation*, a word that is frequently hurled around reapportionment and vote dilution cases. Since the Court has failed to look beyond the realm of abstract definitions of voting behavior and note the variety of observations made in empirical political analysis of voting, it has developed a model of electoral behavior and an approach to redistricting that are inconsistent and incorrect in their assumptions and hypotheses about the nature of voting and group behavior.

The Issues and Questions of Redistricting

The Court has resolved two particular issues: the question of the *justiciability* of reapportionment—not gerrymandering—cases and the standards used to determine the constitutionality of a given reapportionment scheme. The original justification for judicial intervention was set forth in *Baker v. Carr.* Prior to *Baker,* the Court had held that reapportionment was a political question best left to the states and Congress for resolution, because the Constitution embodies no clear standards for determining the validity of schemes of representation and districting.[6] Furthermore, the Court was divided on whether reapportionment disputes were actually guaranty clause disputes in disguise and therefore not justiciable (*Colegrove,* 552).[7]

In *Baker,* a new judicial majority held that reapportionment disputes are justiciable on the grounds that voters in overpopulated districts were denied the equal protection of the laws, because their votes counted less than those of voters in less populated districts.[8] Although the Court extended the equal protection claim to both state legislative and congressional districts (*Wesberry v. Sanders* and *Grey v. Sanders*), it did not suggest a standard for determining the acceptability of apportionment plans until 1964, when it set forth the "one person, one vote" rule in *Reynolds v. Sims.* Equal protection, said Chief Justice Warren, requires that legislative districts have equal populations (568). He noted that some deviations from strict population equality might be tolerated if they were based on rational considerations of state policy (578).[9] Such leniency, however, came to be reserved for state legislative districts only; congressional districts could deviate from strict population equality only for compelling reasons.[10] In setting forth the Fourteenth Amendment as a basis for judicial intervention and establishing the "one person, one vote" rule, the Court sought effectively to protect individual rights. So long as the Court focused only on questions of the dilution of individual votes, it could maintain a straightforward, consistent, Fourteenth Amendment approach to monitoring the drawing of legislative districts. The Court, however, chose not to do so.

Warren also noted in *Reynolds* that equally weighted votes are not necessarily equally effective ones (579, infra). Like-minded voters must vote as blocs in order to have an impact (in addition to just a voice) on the voting and legislative processes. Recognizing this, Warren noted that groups, as well as individuals, must be protected in the drawing of district lines. The question remained as to how they are to be protected. Warren provided no clear answer in *Reynolds,* and no answer has been provided since. The Court has been unable to provide an answer because its approach to problems of apportionment and gerrymandering is founded upon incorrect assumptions about both individual and group voting behavior and questionable or unclear references to constitutional amendments.

The Problems with Analyzing Political Groups

The Court seems to have assumed that equal protection standards to ensure the equality of individual voters can also be used to ensure equality of group representation. This is not the case. To ensure individual voting equality, the

Court has merely to restrain those who draw district lines. But the Court can do little to ensure equality of representation. It can make districts equipopulous, and it can strike down segregative rules that prevent voters who belong to particular groups from voting.[11] The Court cannot ensure that members of a given group will vote in a manner that will enhance the group's chances for representation. Thus, the Court can ensure access and equality at the polls, but only the voters can ensure that a given group is represented.

Therefore the groups that are recognized by the Court must be cohesive enough in their electoral behavior that a given districting scheme could actually impair their attempt at representation. They are only as cohesive, however, as their members are loyal and willing to vote a consistent "group line." The Court cannot ensure such cohesion; it therefore cannot ensure representation, regardless of how fairly districts are drawn or how manageable the Court's standard of fairness may be. The equal protection clause can thus be employed to prevent discrimination against a group by others; it can be used to ensure that a district line does not divide a cohesive group; but it cannot be used to guarantee that the group's members qua voters will all vote in a way that benefits the group.

There is thus a great difference between protecting a "discrete and insular minority" from discrimination and encouraging a group of voters to act as a cohesive unit on election day.[12] *Discrimination* requires the existence of a group of people who have a given trait in common and of other people who will mistreat them for it. *Representation* requires that those same persecuted individuals mobilize. Thus, a persecuted group can be discrete and insular, active or passive. A represented group must be active, regardless of whether it is discrete and insular.

When the Court seeks to protect a persecuted group, it ensures that individual members of the group are treated equally by the government (that is, they receive the equal protection of the laws), regardless of their group membership. It cannot, however, equally protect individuals into mobilizing. In cases of discrimination, the group is thus easily definable as those individuals who *are being denied X* or *persecuted because of Y*. In cases of partisan representation, the group to be represented cannot be defined as such prior to the casting of ballots. We can only anticipate—or, more accurately, try to predict—the outcome of an election and a group's success in mobilizing its members. Nonetheless, the groups whose representation we anticipate might not gain representation. Black Democrats might be more likely to vote for the white Democratic candidate if they feel that he or she can better represent their interests. Similarly, registered members of one party might vote for the other party's candidate if that candidate is more appealing.

When engaging in the predictive enterprise of ensuring representation, the Court must first determine which groups are cohesive and politically relevant enough to play a significant role in the electoral process. This in turn requires that the Court analyze the strength of voter partisanship and loyalty to the groups with which they affiliate. The Court has yet to do so.

There is no question that a cohesive minority group, such as blacks in the South during the reign of Jim Crow, could easily be shut out of the legislative process and denied representation by strategic districting on the part of the majority.[13] As Robert Dixon observed, "The basic premise of political equality, when applied to representative assemblies, must include a concept of political equity at the operative level of allocation of legislative seats as well as the more obvious concept of equal population."[14] Yet blacks are but one group among many that do not necessarily have exclusive membership. Some members of a given racial group may also be Democrats, others Republicans, some urban, some rural, and so on. Whereas Dixon's statement may strike a note of morality and fairness regarding legislative representation, it also presupposes the existence of—or at least the ability to construct—a clear measure by which groups can be differentiated from nongroups.

Justice White's discussion in *Davis v. Bandemer* was predicated on the assumption of clearly defined conceptions of voting behavior, group cohesion, and theories of representation. In focusing upon whether the Court's definition of fairness, as embodied in the equal protection clause of the Fourteenth Amendment, provides a manageable standard, he asserted that the Court has never withdrawn from this area of inquiry and that all groups are fundamentally similar: "The claim is that each political group in a State should have the same chance to elect representatives of its choice as any other political group . . . and [this Court declines] to hold that such claims are never justiciable. That a claim is submitted by a political group, rather than a racial group, does not distinguish it in terms of justiciability" (*Davis*, 124–25). In addition, Justice White stated that the effect of a redistricting plan on any given group's representation should be easily discernible:

> We think it most likely that whenever a legislature redistricts, those responsible for the legislation will know the likely political composition of the new districts and will have a prediction as to whether a particular district is a safe one for a Democratic or Republican candidate or is a competitive district that either candidate might win. . . . As long as redistricting is done by a legislature, it should not be very difficult to prove that the likely political consequences of the reapportionment were intended. (*Davis*, 128–29)

But the likely consequences, intended or not, might not be the actual consequences. The redistricted voters might not vote for the same party as they had previously, for any number of reasons. They might not like or even recognize the new district's candidate, or they might not vote at all.

Justice O'Connor asserted that since the behavior of the individual voters who compose political groups may vary from one election to another, partisan groups can differ in their cohesiveness and composition. More important, no constitutional right exists upon which a group could claim that gerrymandering violated its Fourteenth Amendment rights. The equal protection clause, she asserted, "does not supply judicially manageable standards for resolving purely political gerrymandering claims, and no group right to an equal share of political power was ever intended by the Framers of the Fourteenth Amendment" (*Davis*, 147).

We now see that the debate in *Davis v. Bandemer* embodies several issues. First, there is the question of judicial capacity to create a manageable standard to solve gerrymandering questions.[15] Second, no consensus exists regarding the existence of a group right to representation. Finally, if such a standard and right do exist, which groups are identifiable and cohesive enough to demand protection from a purported gerrymander? Which groups are not so entitled, and why?

In *Davis*, these questions were exposed, but they were addressed only by the minority. If groups cannot be defined consistently, then Justice White's "manageable standard" is virtually impotent because it cannot be applied. If no group right to representation exists, then the gerrymandering question is moot, because only groups can be gerrymandered (individual voters can only be malapportioned). If the group right to representation *does* exist, and assuming that a consistent standard of representational fairness can be created, the Court must still address Justice O'Connor's criticism. Some groups are more monolithic than others; thus, where do we draw the line between groups and nongroups? What criteria should we use to differentiate among them? Unfortunately, the Court's precedents offer little assistance in answering such questions.

The Source of Judicial Confusion: From *Colegrove* to *Gomillion* to *Baker*

The dispute among the justices in *Davis* was rooted in the confusion that manifested itself in the late 1950s and early 1960s. During this time, the Court's membership, along with its attitude toward malapportionment cases, changed drastically.[16] The Court also took a radically different view of the rights at stake in such cases. *Colegrove v. Green, Gomillion v. Lightfoot,* and *Baker v. Carr* indicate the transition that occurred.

The Court's last, and possibly most strident, refusal to become involved in cases of malapportionment or gerrymandering occurred in *Colegrove v. Green.* Justice Frankfurter, speaking for the plurality, asserted that apportionment disputes are political questions and, therefore, not justiciable. Despite gross population inequalities that existed among Illinois's congressional districts, the Court declined to become involved in the dispute, because "it is hostile to a democratic system to involve the judiciary in the politics of the people" (*Colegrove*, 553–54).

The *Colegrove* case was not simply a judicial declination to enter the political thicket. The substantive debate embodied several assumptions about state powers to administer elections, individual voting rights and the effects of malapportionment upon them, and the power of a state to form and redefine the boundaries of its subdivisions. The Justices diverged widely in their views on these issues. Frankfurter's opinion met with strong dissent. Justice Hugo Black, along with Justices William C. Douglas and Frank Murphy, asserted that despite the political nature of reapportionment questions—and despite the states' constitutional authority to administer elections as they see fit—the state's power to define legislative districts is not plenary. No constitutional power can be exercised at the expense of the rights of individual voters. Black wrote: "While the Constitution contains no express provision requiring that congressional election districts established by the States must contain approximately equal populations, the constitutionally guaranteed right to vote and the right to have one's vote counted clearly imply the policy that state election systems, no matter what their form, should be designed to give approximately equal weight to each vote cast" (*Colegrove*, 571).

The two justices thus approached the reapportionment problem from radically different perspectives. Frankfurter envisioned a plenary state power to draw and define subdivisions, acknowledged no Fourteenth Amendment problem or violation, and, as a result, saw no basis for judicial intervention. Black perceived a more restricted state power, which was restrained by the Fourteenth Amendment's protection of individual rights. Since Black believed that malapportionment and vote dilution are infringements of such rights, he asserted that the Court was bound to intervene.

Neither acknowledged the existence of a cohesive group of underrepresented voters. Both opinions focused only upon the rights of individual voters. "Underrepresented voters in certain parts of Illinois" were not regarded as a "discrete or insular" group that could easily be shut out of the legislative process.[17] Black did mention that in drawing district lines, states cannot "discriminate against some groups to favor others" (*Colegrove*, 574). To give "all the people an equally effective voice in electing their representatives [is] essential under a free government." However, he did not state whether these underrepresented Illinois voters constituted a group that actually could suffer discrimination. Accordingly, in *Colegrove*, several key points were made that provided the basis for the judicial dispute: First, states have the right to draw district lines as provided by Article 1, sec. 4, and to form and redefine municipal corporations as reserved to the states in the Tenth Amendment. Second, any dispute arising in the apportionment of voting districts was to be resolved by either the states or Congress as stated similarly in Article 1, Section 4. Third, if there had been a violation of the equal protection clause as a result of the dilution of the votes of individuals, the Court could have intervened, but only a minority of the justices (Blackmun, Murphy, and Douglas) regarded vote dilution as such a violation. Finally, no reference was made to the Fifteenth Amendment because

(1.) plaintiffs did not assert that they had been denied their vote; they claimed only that they had been denied equal treatment; (2.) this unequal treatment as a result of malapportionment was not regarded as a violation of the Fourteenth or Fifteenth Amendments because dilution, even if it were unconstitutional, is not tantamount to denial (569, 568).

Although Frankfurter's opinion prevailed, it did so only because Justice Wiley Blount Rutledge concurred in the result. He agreed that the Court should stay out of reapportionment disputes at that time, only because he was unable to find a basis upon which to construe an equitable remedy (565). Accordingly, he said that the Court should avoid entanglement in this political thicket: "The right here is not absolute. And the cure sought may be worse than the disease" (566).

Despite Rutledge's reservations about the Court's capacity to resolve such disputes, fourteen years later, in *Gomillion v. Lightfoot,* Justice Frankfurter wrote the opinion in which the Court asserted that Alabama would have to redraw once again the border of the City of Tuskegee, because the newly drawn line effectively excluded blacks from participating in the city's politics by zoning them into the surrounding areas. Unlike *Colegrove, Gomillion* involved an alleged denial of voting rights under the Fifteenth Amendment. Justice Frankfurter and the Court accordingly saw a marked difference between dealing, on the one hand, with abstract issues of vote dilution and addressing, on the other, unconstitutional legislation "solely concerned with segregating white and colored voters by fencing Negro citizens out of town so as to deprive them of their pre-existing municipal vote" (*Gomillion,* 341).

There are significant differences in the circumstances of the two cases. Whereas the Illinois legislature had simply failed to alter district boundaries in response to population shifts, Alabama had created a "strangely irregular twenty-eight-sided figure" in order to prevent blacks from residing, and therefore voting, in Tuskegee (ibid.). The Court also restated its position regarding the limits of state sovereignty. In *Gomillion,* the Court maintained that states do not have unlimited discretion in drawing subdivision boundaries (344–45). *Colegrove* allowed states significantly more discretion in deciding when *not to draw* congressional district boundaries.[18] Thus, in *Gomillion,* the Court considered the key factors differently: (1) the state has the right to determine municipal boundaries, but (2) it cannot exercise this right to the detriment of individual constitutional rights; in this specific case, it cannot be exercised in such a way as to deny or abridge the right to vote. The next step in the Court's argument is questionable, as it assumes that the right to vote was, in fact, abridged on account of race: (3) the redrawing of the municipal limits of Tuskegee so as to exclude blacks from city residence violates the Fifteenth Amendment because it is tantamount to denying their right to vote (347).

The problem here is that the *right to vote* was not denied, only the *right to vote in Tuskegee.*[19] Accordingly, the redrawing of Tuskegee did not violate the

Fifteenth Amendment. It violated only the Fourteenth Amendment because it served to segregate blacks and whites *but only insofar as the boundary of Tuskegee was concerned.* The Court never clearly stated the difference between the two cases. Justice Frankfurter differentiated between them this way:

> [*Colegrove*] involved a complaint of discriminatory apportionment of congressional districts. The appellants in *Colegrove* complained only of a dilution of the strength of their votes as a result of legislative inaction over a course of many years. The petitioners here [in *Gomillion*] complain that affirmative legislative action deprives them of their votes and the consequent advantages that the ballot affords. *When a legislature thus singles out a readily isolated segment of a racial minority for special discriminatory treatment, it violates the Fifteenth Amendment.* In no case involving unequal weight in voting distribution that has come before the Court did the decision sanction a differentiation on racial lines whereby approval was given to unequivocal withdrawal of the vote solely from colored citizens. Apart from all else, these considerations lift this controversy out of the so-called "political" arena and into the conventional sphere of constitutional litigation. (346–47, emphasis added)

However, this opinion does not explain how denial of the opportunity to vote in Tuskegee constituted a wholesale denial of the franchise. The motives behind the state legislature's separation of the races were rather obvious. By fencing blacks out of Tuskegee, the state had designedly sought to prevent them from voting in municipal elections. As Frankfurter himself noted, this redrawing of the city's boundary was an "impairment of voting rights . . . cloaked in the garb of the realignment of political subdivisions" (345).

The Court did not emphasize the racially unique nature of the situation in Tuskegee; nor did it address the questions raised by Justice Charles Evans Whittaker, who, in his concurring opinion, asserted that the case was better decided as a question of equal protection, not vote denial. He explained: "It would seem to follow that one's right to vote in Division A is not abridged by a redistricting that places his residence in Division B *if* he there enjoys the same voting privileges as all others in that Division, even though the redistricting was done by the State for the purpose of placing a racial group of citizens in Division B rather than A" (349, emphasis in original). If, for example, the city had been arbitrarily split in two, there would not have been Fifteenth Amendment grounds upon which to challenge the state's actions. In such a case, those voters (black and white) who had been cut out of a city would not have comprised a distinct racial minority.

The only way the Court could have regarded the redrawing of Tuskegee as a denial of the right to vote would have been to assume that (1) blacks were a cohesive group capable of voting as a majority in Tuskegee, (2) they voted as such in Tuskegee, (3) cutting them out of Tuskegee did in fact dilute the power of their vote qua a group, and (4) this dilution of the power of their group vote was tantamount to the denial or abridgment of the franchise to individual blacks.[20] This equation, however, would have contradicted Frankfurter's assertion in *Colegrove* that dilution as such was nonjusticiable.

Whether intended or not, Frankfurter's *Gomillion* opinion, along with Whittaker's concurrence, effectively laid the groundwork for future group claims to representation, because his attempt to use the Fifteenth Amendment in order to remedy a clear Fourteenth Amendment violation suggested the existence of a group right to representation. In fact, the *Gomillion* decision was actually alluded to in later cases as an expression of the unconstitutionality of vote dilution.[21]

Two years later, in *Baker v. Carr*, Justice Frankfurter reasserted his political thicket argument, but this time he spoke for a dissenting minority. Justice Brennan, who spoke for the Court, held that claims of malapportionment qua claims of vote impairment were justiciable under the equal protection clause. He noted that four justices (Black, Murphy, Douglas, and Rutledge) actually had agreed upon this in *Colegrove*, despite reservations that *Colegrove* presented a viable constitutional claim (201) and cited *Gomillion* as another example of judicial intervention in other cases of vote deprivation (229).

Although Brennan's argument was based strictly on the Fourteenth Amendment, he never alluded to the distinction Frankfurter had made between the presence of a Fifteenth Amendment remedy in *Gomillion* and the unavailability of a Fourteenth Amendment remedy in *Colegrove* (*Baker*, 237). In a separate concurrence, Justice Douglas asserted that "the question is, may a state weigh the vote in one county or district more heavily than it weighs the vote in another?" Answering his own question, he explained: "The traditional test under the Equal Protection Clause has been whether a State has made 'an invidious discrimination,' as it does when it selects 'a particular race or nationality for oppressive treatment.' . . . Universal equality is not the test; there is room for weighting. . . . The prohibition of the Equal Protection Clause goes no further than the invidious discrimination" (244–45, citations omitted). Was the Court equating the discrimination in *Colegrove* with that in *Gomillion*?

For there to have been an "invidious discrimination," there must have been a persecuted group. One could argue that invidious discrimination requires only the persecution of individuals. However, for a group to be persecuted, several individuals who are group members must be regarded as somehow being injured. In gerrymandering, it is necessary to show that all group members (as counted by the plaintiff) actually behave in a manner that substantiates the plaintiff's assertion that the group is being persecuted.

If the blacks in Tuskegee had actually been divided over certain issues and therefore did not normally act as one cohesive group, plaintiffs in *Gomillion* would have been hard-pressed to prove that the blacks had been denied their fair representational opportunity, since it could not be argued that there existed a large, cohesive group of black voters. Instead, there would have been several black political groups that did not act in unison. Doubtless, black individuals could have claimed that they had been treated unfairly because only blacks had been cut out of the city. However, unfairness to individuals under these circumstances would not have been tantamount to unfair treatment of the group to which they are said to belong. Thus, group cohesion is a necessary component of a gerrymander claim but not of a Fourteenth Amendment claim of discrimination.

In *Colegrove* and in *Gomillion*'s discussion of *Colegrove*, underrepresented voters in Illinois were not regarded as persecuted groups. In these cases, the Illinois voters were regarded or referred to only as individuals whose votes had been diluted and had therefore not been treated equally. The blacks in *Gomillion* had been so singled out, but their right to vote had not been denied. Thus, they had an equal protection claim, despite the fact that the Court addressed their claim as if they had been denied their Fifteenth Amendment right to vote. In *Baker,* Douglas neglected to explain how a *Colegrove* situation, which had been brushed off in *Gomillion* as "only . . . a dilution of the strength of [plaintiffs'] votes as a result of legislative inaction over a course of many years," was, in *Baker,* as egregious and unconstitutional as the invidious "affirmative legislative action" in *Gomillion.*[22]

In *Colegrove,* there was no recognizable group; therefore there was no invidious discrimination and no equal protection violation, because vote dilution was not regarded as invidious discrimination. In *Gomillion,* there was neither vote dilution nor vote denial, but there was invidious discrimination and the consequent denial of the right to vote in Tuskegee, which was equated with wholesale denial of the franchise.

In *Baker,* invidious discrimination was alleged when only dilution had occurred. Now, however, individuals with diluted votes were regarded as a group that could be discriminated against in the same way that the blacks had been cut out of Tuskegee. The former's dilution was as egregious as the latter's denial of the franchise, even though the Court failed to explain exactly who constituted the diluted group.

Had the Warren Court now come to regard vote dilution as invidious discrimination against clearly defined groups of diluted voters? Were voters entitled not only to equally weighted votes but also to district apportionment lines drawn so that *any* group to which they belonged and which sought representation in a legislature would have a fair opportunity to be represented?[23] If so, on which constitutional referent was the group representation claim based, and what sort of a group was entitled to representation? In *Gomillion,* the group was the black community, which had been denied the opportunity to establish itself as a local majority. But what were the ties that bound underrepresented voters in Tennessee in the *Baker* case?

In his concurrence, Justice Tom Campbell Clark cited *MacDougal v. Green* in order to explain that certain interests might be disadvantaged in a given representation scheme and that states might rationally and constitutionally deviate from equipopulous districts in order to give the weaker interests the chance to be heard. "It would be strange indeed, and doctrinaire, for this Court, applying such broad constitutional concepts as due process and equal protection of the laws, to deny a State the power to assure a *proper* diffusion of political initiative as between its thinly populated counties and those having concentrated masses, *in view of the fact that the latter have practical opportunities for exerting their political weight at the polls not available to the former"* (*Baker*, 252, citing *MacDougal,* Clark's emphasis). If there can be a *proper* diffusion of influence among communities of interest, there must also be an *improper* diffusion; but this raises the question: What was the difference between the plaintiffs in *Baker* and those in *Colegrove?* The Court never answered. Clark noted only that the *Baker* majority appeared to hold "at least *sub silentio,* that an invidious discrimination is present, but it remands to the three-judge court for it to make what is certain to be that formal determination" (*Baker*, 261). Thus, the Court was unable to decide clearly upon a working definition of *equal* and *representation.*[24] The result was a concurrent failure to ask, as Robert Dixon states, "the true question: [equality of representation for equal numbers of] *what* population—*what* people—what spokesmen for *what* interests?" (224, emphasis in original).

The Court did not consider whether other groups could be segregated in the same way that blacks had been in *Gomillion.* The *Baker* opinion begged the questions: (1) Were the underrepresented voters discriminated against qua a class (as was the case in *Gomillion*) and therefore entitled to Fourteenth Amendment protection? (2) Was the dilution of the vote in this case tantamount to denial? and (3) Was the set of individuals who happened to be living in an underrepresented district now also regarded a cohesive group? The argument could be made that the Court seemed to be equating the class of blacks who, because they were cut out of the city, were disenfranchised with the class of voters in underrepresented district X in Tennessee. But if this were the case, why weren't they equivalent to the underrepresented voters in Illinois? The Court had clearly overturned *Colegrove* without explaining why it had done so.[25]

The Unanswered Questions

Without discussing this inconsistency, the Court proceeded to develop its jurisprudence upon a model of representation and group behavior grounded on several questionable assumptions. First, the Court came to interpret the Fourteenth and Fifteenth Amendments together as creating an implicit group right to representation as a function of the explicit individual right to vote. This, however, for our purposes, is simply a matter of interpretation. Whether or not the framers of the two amendments ever intended that groups should have some representational entitlement is not relevant to this discussion. Even if such a right were proved to exist, the Court still would be left with the problem of distinguishing and measuring the nature of divers social groups and deciding which aggregations of voters are monolithic enough to be regarded as a groups qua cohesive, corporate associations, as opposed to more loosely defined classes of individuals. Instead, the Court, prior to the *Davis* decision, had come to equate all groups (*Karcher v. Daggett,* 750, Stevens, J., dissenting).

Second, by overlooking this distinction between association and class, the Court had no basis on which to consider that some groups might be more monolithic than others. Blacks might be more cohesive than whites, but could it be argued that they were more cohesive than Tennessee Republicans or under-represented voters in Tennessee District X? What if the few black Republicans in Tennessee district X felt stronger ties to the black Democratic candidate than to the white Republican candidate? Republicans would then be acting as Democrats because they were black. The Court's logic overlooked the possibility that individuals might hold multiple group affiliations and, therefore, could neither be classified neatly into one single category, nor counted on to vote consistently as members of one category instead of the other.

Third, the Court's blurring of the distinction between group and individual rights and between classes and associations led to its similar inability to distinguish between the two types of cases that arose in the context of redistricting disputes. On the one hand, cases such as *Baker v. Carr* and *Reynolds v. Sims* addressed issues of malapportionment and equality of individual voting power in voting districts. Other cases such as *Fortson v. Dorsey, Whitcomb v. Chavis* and *Thornburg v. Gingles* addressed problems of group representation and, to some extent, gerrymandering.[26]

The former set of cases addresses a fairly straightforward issue: How equally balanced are the respective populations of a given set of legislative districts? A calculator or slide rule could serve to answer such a question, leaving the Court to address such further questions as How much disparity among district populations is tolerable? and Can there exist a *de minimis* standard of population disparity, beneath which constitutionality will be assumed?[27] The latter set is far more complex, because it requires that the Court attempt not only to balance the voting impact of diverse political groups but also to establish a coherent standard by which a group may be defined and distinguished from other aggregations of voters.

The former focuses on the one person, one vote principle and can easily be derived from Chief Justice Warren's assertion in *Reynolds* that "the fact that an individual lives here or there is not a legitimate reason for overweighting or diluting the efficacy of his vote" (567).[28] The second set, which involves the question of group rights to representation, can just as easily be derived from the fact that "fair and effective representation for all citizens is concededly the basic aim of legislative reapportionment" (565–66). Gradually, these two strains of thought became intertwined, resulting in the Court's attempts to answer questions of group vote dilution. The Court entered the group representation thicket without first deciding which groups were entitled to representation and how to differentiate groups from nongroups.

The Exacerbation of Judicial Confusion: *Reynolds v. Sims*

Virtually any discussion of the existence of a group right to representation ultimately boils down to how one interprets the following passage from Chief Justice Warren's opinion in *Reynolds v. Sims*.

> Representative government is in essence self-government through the medium of elected representatives of the people, and each and every citizen has an inalienable right to *full* and *effective participation* in the political processes of his State's legislative bodies. Most citizens can achieve this participation only as qualified voters through the election of legislators to represent them. *Full and effective participation by all citizens in state government requires, therefore, that each citizen have an equally effective voice in the election of members of his state legislature.* Modern and viable state government needs, and the Constitution demands, no less.
>
> Logically, in a society ostensibly grounded on representative government, it would seem reasonable that a majority of the people of a State could elect a majority of that State's legislators. To conclude differently, and to sanction minority control of state legislative bodies, would appear to deny majority rights in a way that far surpasses any possible denial of minority rights that might otherwise be thought to result. (565, emphasis added)

At this point in his opinion, Justice Warren seemed to be stating simply that every vote should carry the same weight and that majority rule is the basis for our scheme of representation. However, he qualified these statements almost immediately:

> The concept of equal protection has been traditionally viewed as requiring the uniform treatment of persons standing in the same relation to the governmental action questioned or challenged. With respect to the allocation of legislative representation, all voters, as citizens of a State, stand in the same relation regardless of where they live. Any suggested criteria for the differentiation of citizens are insufficient to justify any discrimination, as to the weight of their votes, *unless relevant to the permissible purposes of legislative apportionment*. Since the achieving of *fair and effective representation for all citizens is concededly the basic aim of legislative apportionment*, we conclude that the Equal Protection Clause guarantees *the opportunity for equal participation for all voters in the election of state legislators*. (565–66, emphasis added)

This passage appears to intermingle two different patterns of thought. On the one hand, all citizens' votes are to weigh the same. On the other, some citizens can be treated differently if the basis of the differential treatment is a function of a legitimate state objective.[29] Then again, Justice Warren alluded to group factors, such as race, in order to assert that the constitution does not tolerate vote dilution. "Diluting the weight of votes because of place of residence impairs basic constitutional rights under the Fourteenth Amendment just as mush as invidious discriminations based upon factors such as race . . . or economic status. . . . Our constitutional system amply provides for the protection of minorities by means other than giving them majority control of state legislatures" (Reynolds, 566). Warren's argument, which began as a discussion of the protection of *individual* rights, finished with suggestions about the conditioning of those rights by the individual's *group* membership. Thus, the Chief Justice left readers and future justices with the responsibility for interpreting this murky precedent.

Nearly three decades have passed since Reynolds, and disagreement still persists regarding the proper interpretation of this passage. In Davis v. Bandemer, Justice White read this passage as one that "surely indicates the justiciability of claims going to the adequacy of representation in state legislatures" (124). Accordingly, he maintained that in formulating the one man, one vote standard, "the Court characterized the question posed by election districts of disparate size as an issue of fair representation" (123). Yet, as Justice O'Connor pointed out in her concurrence and Justice White conceded, Baker and Reynolds asserted an individual right to a vote that was not arbitrarily diluted.[30]

The inconsistencies and disagreements in Davis are firmly rooted in similar inconsistencies and disagreements in the precedents cited therein, which are further confused by the murkiness of the dicta in Colegrove, Gomillion, and Baker. The Court has been unclear about the connection between the individual and group rights or to what extent they may overlap or be distinct.

On this issue, Warren's opinion in Reynolds is especially unclear. Justice White read it as an assertion that there is a broad nexus between individual and group rights and that the Court has the capacity (or at least the responsibility to try) to solve questions of representational equality (Davis, 124). The opinion may appear to suggest as well that states may have legitimate reasons in some cases to malapportion districts. It might, as Robert Dixon states, appear to assert that the Court will tolerate nothing short of strict population equality.[31] Finally, one could read the passage, as Justice O'Connor did, as an assertion that the question of equality focuses only on individual rights and that group representation is irrelevant (Davis, 148, O'Connor, J., concurring).

Despite the fact that Warren's opinion could arguably be interpreted in any of these ways, the debate that has developed within and as a result of the Davis opinion does not address a second and no less important aspect of the issue. Once the justices arrive at a consensus about which rights are to be recognized and protected, how is the Court to go about resolving or remedying claims of unequal treatment? To adjust malapportioned districts we need only to shift voters. In order to remedy gerrymanders, however, we need to shift members of cohesive groups.[32] The argument could, of course, be made that *redistricted voters* compose a distinct and definable class of voters. But the Court has yet to explain clearly how the redistricting of voters establishes some sort of associational bond among them.

Throughout the debate and between *Reynolds* and *Davis,* there seems to exist a tacit assumption that group equality can easily be derived from individual equality and that groups (as well as parts of groups) can be shifted just as easily as individual voters. As Dixon notes,

> It was assumed unquestioningly that "equal representation" magically arises from creating districts of equal population. The term *"equal population districts"* denotes a verifiable objective concept. But *"equal representation"* is a highly subjective term connoting a hoped-for result. The result may be promoted or defeated by a congeries of factors, some objective, like "equal population districts," and some subjective, like gerrymandering. The Court's equating of the two concepts is a classic example of moving from an objective concept to a highly subjective concept without noting the shift.[33] (emphasis in original)

This assumption that population equality could somehow lead to equality of group representation caused the Court to confuse and equate the weighing of individual voters with the measuring and comparing of groups of voters. Dixon states: "In *franchise cases,* a voter has an absolute right to equality. *Representation cases* are not franchise cases. But the instinctive inclination in many briefs and opinions to treat the two as one fostered a strong tendency to import the absolute equality principle, which is necessary as a democratic postulate in the franchise cases, into the quite different field of representation cases" (181, emphasis in original). Thus, the Court embarked on its post-*Reynolds* adventure in redistricting (1) amid a confusion of individual and group rights, (2) assuming falsely that groups are as monolithic and therefore as easily redistrictable and representable as individual voters, and (3) despite an absence of clear criteria for differentiating among different types of groups. In subsequent redistricting cases, the Court attempted to clarify the confusion and to address varieties of groups and group behavior.

The Development of the Judicial Model after *Reynolds*

In *Fortson v. Dorsey,* the first multimember district case, the Court shifted its focus completely in order to address the effect of a gerrymandered—not necessarily malapportioned—district. No individual voting rights were at stake, nor were individual votes diluted. Instead, the question of individual equality was subsumed in order to focus upon group political behavior and the possibilities of gerrymandering. The Court explained: "It might well be the case that designedly or otherwise, a multimember constituency apportionment scheme, under the circumstances of a particular case, would operate to minimize or cancel out the voting strength of racial or political elements of the voting population" (439). Such could be the case even if districts all had the same population.

In 1969, Robert Dixon asserted that the Court had subordinated this concern within the context of ensuring absolute population equality.[34] He pointed to Justice Brennan's opinion in *Kirkpatrick v. Preisler* as the quintessential example of the Court's failure to acknowledge the fact that the political strength of groups could be nullified even in the most equally apportioned districts. "Equal representation for equal numbers of people is a principle designed to prevent debasement of voting power and diminution of access to elected representatives. Toleration of even small deviations detracts from these purposes. Therefore, the command of Art. I, §2 . . . permits only the limited population variances which are unavoidable despite a good faith effort to achieve absolute equality, or for which justification is shown" (531). Dixon contended, however, that individual voters are not isolated. They function as members of groups that organize for political action. Accordingly, insofar as groups are aggregations of individuals, they are entitled to Fourteenth Amendment protection of their collective rights to undiluted suffrage.

The Court did, in fact, begin to address and employ Dixon's perception of group representation one year later, in *Whitcomb v. Chavis*. However the Court, as well as Dixon, sought to address and remedy the problems of group representation without first addressing and observing the relationships between individual voters, the associations in which they choose to participate, and the classes to which social scientists say they belong. Instead, the Court entered into this political fray by assuming that all groups are uniformly cohesive and tend to function as unitary, rational actors. The Court's model of group voting was derived from situations involving extreme racial tension and was therefore not necessarily applicable to other groups in other areas.[35]

Whitcomb v. Chavis and Justice Douglas's Definition of Groups

In *Whitcomb*, Justice White's opinion for the Court asserted that multimember state legislative districts were not, in and of themselves, unconstitutional. In this case, the plaintiffs had asserted that the multimember district discriminated against poor blacks living in the ghetto area of Marion County, Indiana. The Court rejected the plaintiffs' assertion that "any group with distinctive interests must be represented in legislative halls if it is numerous enough to command at least one seat and represents a majority living in an area sufficiently compact to constitute a single member district" (156). Since ghetto-area voters had supported candidates from both parties in the past, the Court reasoned that they must have been at least partially satisfied (and therefore represented) in past contests (151–52). If the ghetto voters had been sufficiently unified, they might have been able to defeat a candidate in their district by concentrating their support. The Court ruled that the issue was getting out the vote, not the electoral bias of multimember districts (152–53).

Justice White and the majority further maintained that the mere fact that the ghetto was sufficiently populous and compact to be regarded as a political group did not serve to guarantee any representation qua a group in the legislature. Such an approach to systems of representation, he said, "would make it difficult to reject claims of Democrats, Republicans, or members of any political organization in Marion County who live in what would be safe districts in a single-member district system, but who in one year or another, or year after year, are submerged in a one-sided multi-member district vote" (156). Here, the Court seemed to reject Dixon's complaints regarding group representation in single-member plurality elections. In fact, Justice White's opinion echoes Dixon's assertion that, functionally, "there is no such thing as 'equal representation' in a district system of electing legislators," due to the built-in discounting of the loser's votes.[36]

Although the Court's opinion denied that all groups are entitled to representation, it suggested that groups seeking to be represented can in fact be measured and related along a scale of cohesiveness, political salience, and so on (*Whitcomb*, 158). This abstract assumption led the Court to focus on which groups *should* be represented, instead of seeking first to determine if groups generally could be measured and related and their representation therefore balanced.

In his dissent, Justice Douglas asserted that groups can be identified and measured, and he set forth his criteria for drawing districts so as to ensure the fair representation of all political groups.

> The question of the gerrymander is the other half of *Reynolds v. Sims*. . . . Fair representation of voters in a legislative assembly—one man, one vote—would seem to require (1) substantial equality of population within each district and (2) the avoidance of district lines that weigh the power of one race more heavily than another. The latter can be done—and is done—by astute drawing of district lines that makes the district either heavily Democratic or heavily Republican as the case may be. Lines may be drawn so as to make the voice of one racial group weak or strong, as the case may be. (176–77, citations omitted)

Thus, Douglas, as well as White, chose to inquire into only the nature of group rights—not the nature of political groups. Their discussion of groups made sense only if individual members of a given group shared a uniform fidelity to that group and therefore, for all practical purposes, could be assumed by the

Court to be members of a monolithic entity. The Court was toying with the abstract idea of rights to fairness in group representation, without providing any evidence to prove that individual voting behavior substantiated their assumptions about the unity and predictability of group behavior.

The Court, like Dixon, assumed that because two different groups were composed of individuals with equal rights to vote, the two groups could be measured and represented almost proportionally, despite the fact that we employ a district system of representation. Dixon observed:

Though we have tended to talk primarily of district elections and majority rule, our central concern is *proportionality in political representation*. Groups, and coalitions of groups, including the majority coalition itself, are to be heard in rough *proportion* to their popular strength in the deliberative-governance process. Of course, a district system tends to "pay off" only to large groups. Only a large group has much prospect of obtaining a plurality and winning a seat, thus making political parties the dominant groups. To an important degree, however, subgroups such as ethnic minorities, occupational classifications, and economic class categories tend to identify more with one party than another. They thus receive their political representation, at least in a rough way, through one political party or the other; the concern for "proportionality" continues. A set of legislative districts—whether or not "equal" in population—in which a political party consistently polls close to 40 percent of the vote but seldom musters more than 20 percent of the seats, denies effective political representation in terms of legislative bargaining power to the minority (or to the set of minorities that make up the majority).[37] (emphasis in original)

Dixon does not discuss whether all groups are equatable or interchangeable in their behavioral patterns. Groups do not always stick faithfully to their respective majority or minority coalition. Even if the group does so in general, individual members of the group may split ranks and vote for the opposite coalition or another minority. In addition, one must question the logic of Dixon's argument, which, here, sounds like an endorsement of virtual representation.

It can be argued that a single-member district system is purposefully geared to ensuring the existence of a governing coalition and does not necessarily serve to produce an assembly that is a representative microcosm of every social group or rift. If this were the case, the need for proportional virtual representation would be irrelevant, because the systems' focus would be to form governments by forcing coalitions to unite, not to create a microcosm of the country's every political tendency. The Court may have decided at some point that proportional representation is the more desirable scheme, but there are no grounds upon which to assert that proportional representation is any more in keeping with constitutional tenets than single-member plurality representation.

Furthermore, Dixon's vicarious representation argument in his call for virtual proportional representation is not necessarily inconsistent with a single-member system. Just as one could argue that the two parties vicariously represent all of the social factions, so one could argue that social factions are so diffuse that their membership has no sharp boundaries; as a result, different members of a given faction could be members of different parties. Also, in light of the prevalence of ticket splitting in the United States, one could argue that, despite partisan control of the seats at a particular level of the federal system, the government represents the interests of the entire society, because at any given time a significant number of voters vote for both parties in the same election.

Of course, it would be difficult to argue that whites vicariously represented blacks in the South during and after the Civil War. But it would be similarly difficult to argue that every member of a group, whose leadership chooses to ally with one party or the other, embodies all of the views that are espoused and held by its elite leadership.[38] Even if a group were sufficiently numerous, compact, and cohesive to constitute a majority in a single-member district, there is no guarantee that all members of the group would support the same party. One need look only as far as the increase in ticket splitting and the decreasing length of presidential coattails to see that partisan loyalty can vary within elections, as well as across eras.

Since the ghetto residents in *Whitcomb* did seem to constitute a cohesive group large enough to create a majority in a single-member legislative district, it could be said that they were entitled to some sort of representation in the state legislature. On the other hand, it may be the case that the ghetto occupies only a small minority position in a congressional district. Accordingly, the same logic might indicate that the ghetto was not entitled to representation at the congressional level.

One could allude to Dixon's argument and state that, in such a case, the ghetto residents, since they tend to vote en bloc for the Democrats—as they did in state legislative elections in *Whitcomb*—are entitled to proportional Democratic representation in the congressional delegation, to ensure their fair share of virtual representation (see *Whitcomb*, 152). However, the Democratic state legislator might disagree completely with the positions of his congressman. The ghetto residents, who support the state legislator, might therefore vote for the Republican congressional candidate.

Neither Dixon, who recommended the use of bipartisan apportionment procedures to ensure large-group (and therefore, vicarious little-group) representation, nor the Court ever addressed the possibility that group behavior may vary significantly within a single election or from year to year.[39] Instead, the Court proceeded to develop and apply a model of group behavior that assumed an internal group cohesiveness, a hierarchical cohesiveness among subgroups and allied larger groups, and a distinct and unique membership of all groups.

Gaffney v. Cummings and the Employment of Dixon's Model

One year after *Whitcomb*, the Court approved Connecticut's state legislative apportionment plan, which embodied Dixon's bipartisan method of gerrymandering. The state had employed this method to ensure that the partisan membership of the legislature approximated the partisan composition of the electorate, as determined by the last three statewide elections (*Gaffney*, 738). Instead of addressing the more common problem involving equally populated districts that seemed to dilute the strength of a particular minority, the Court now confronted a situation in which intentionally gerrymandered districts of unequal population had been employed to ensure the proportional representation of both major political parties. Originally the Court had stated that a scheme that creates districts of equal population might be invalid because it fences out a racial group "so as to deprive them of their pre-existing municipal vote" (*Gomillion*, 341). In *Gaffney*, the Court argued that a bipartisan gerrymander, which effectively *fenced in* the two major parties, was justifiable, because seeking to achieve a proportionality of party strength was deemed to be a legitimate state interest (*Gaffney*, 752). The Court, however, never addressed the potentially deleterious effect that such a scheme might have on new or third parties.

Justice White noted that, in Connecticut, the Democrats and Republicans were "the only two parties in the State large enough to elect legislators from discernible geographic areas" (ibid.). But what would the Court have ruled if the discernible geographic districts submerged ghetto residents to such an extent that they could never be fairly represented? Despite the inherent cohesiveness of any given group, if the discernible geographic districts were too big such interests would not be regarded as politically salient.

Although this gerrymander-inspired malapportionment of districts was done in a benevolent manner, the Court never stated how it could be certain that the two parties, which were the only dominant groups at that time, would endure to the exclusion of other political groups. Which smaller groups could be regarded as potentially larger groups and therefore entitled to consideration in the districting process? New York, for example, has had as many as four parties (Democrats, Republicans, Liberals, and Conservatives) registered at the state level. Had the Court's dominant-group rationale been applied at some time when the Democrats and Republicans were the only discernible groups, parties such as the Libertarians in New York might not now exist.

The Court thus crossed several levels of electoral analysis without stopping to answer questions that such analytical jumps might present. It assumed that because individuals could be classified as members of a given group, they would remain loyal to that group, regardless of the circumstances. Group cohesion was assumed, yet neither fluidity of individual voter choice nor the possibility of one's membership in more than one group was considered when addressing the nature of a group's cohesion. The Court asserted that, in theory, groups had to be represented; but it could not provide a measure to ensure their representation in practice.

Karcher v. Daggett and the Festering of Dixon's Oversights

In *Karcher v. Daggett* (1983), the Court, led this time by Justice Brennan, reasserted the strict population equality standard (for congressional districts) and ruled that the New Jersey districting plan, which had an average population variance of 0.1384 percent, was invalid, because the state legislature had rejected other plans with smaller population deviations. Contradicting his demand for strict population equality in *Kirkpatrick v. Preisler*,[40] Justice Brennan stated that, as in *Gaffney*, the Court was willing to defer to legitimate state legislative policy goals (none of which were present in *Karcher*) in the redistricting process

> so long as they are consistent with constitutional norms, even if they require small differences in the population of congressional districts. . . . Any number of consistently applied legislative policies might justify some variance, including, for instance, making districts compact, respecting municipal boundaries, preserving the cores of prior districts, and avoiding contests between incumbent Representatives. As long as the criteria are nondiscriminatory . . . these are all legitimate objectives that on a proper showing could justify minor population deviations. (*Karcher*, 740, citations omitted)

This opinion begs several questions. How, for example, could the blatantly bipartisan gerrymander in *Gaffney* be regarded as "nondiscriminatory"? Although the Court asserted that the Democrats and Republicans were the only relevant groups in Connecticut (and therefore, their bipartisan plan was not *mutually* discriminatory), they are also the two major parties in New Jersey. Nonetheless, the deviation of less than a percentage point (among congressional districts) was overruled, while the seven-point deviation in Connecticut's legislative districts was sustained.[41]

Despite the apparent inconsistency in its decisions, the Court maintained that there was an inherent logic to its adjudication: "Judicial standards under the Equal Protection Clause are well developed and familiar, and it has been open to courts since the enactment of the Fourteenth Amendment to determine, if on the particular facts they must, that a discrimination reflects *no* policy, but simply arbitrary and capricious action" (*Baker*, 226, emphasis in original). But if standards are so clear, why has the Court been unable to establish any semblance of a consistent constitutional doctrine? Racial gerrymanders are not permissible; bipartisan gerrymanders are tolerable if motivated by constitutionally justified means. Some population deviations are permissible, but others are not. Black ghetto residents can be submerged within a district but only if their opportunity for representation is not eradicated. The two major parties can fence themselves into a districting plan (thereby eradicating the chances for other political groups to be represented) if, in the Court's opinion, they are the only relevant groups in the state. However, this rule applied only to Connecticut's state legislative districts—not New Jersey's congressional districts.

Justice John Paul Stevens's concurrence in *Karcher* offers what might be the clearest example of the reasons for confusion and lack of clarity. He referred to *Gomillion v. Lightfoot* as an equal protection case, despite the fact that the dicta he cites from that case make explicit allusions to the Fifteenth Amendment (*Karcher*, 748). He explains this reinterpretation of murky precedents thus:

> Although the [*Gomillion*] Court explicitly rested its decision on the Fifteenth Amendment, the analysis in Justice Whittaker's concurring opinion—like Justice Clark's in *Wesberry*—is equally coherent. . . . Moreover, the Court has subsequently treated *Gomillion* as though it had been decided on equal protection grounds. . . .
>
> *Gomillion* involved complete geographical exclusion of a racially identified group. But in case after case arising under the Equal Protection Clause the Court has suggested that "dilution" of the voting strength of cognizable *political* as well as racial groups may be unconstitutional. (748–49, citations omitted; emphasis in original)

If there is any doubt that members of the Court were coming to regard all groups—racial or political—as virtually interchangeable, Stevens erased it later in a footnote.

> If the Tuskegee map in *Gomillion* had excluded virtually all Republicans rather than blacks from the city limits, the Constitution would also have been violated. Professor Tribe gives a comparably egregious numerical hypothetical:
>
> "For example, if a jurisdiction consisting of 540 Republicans and 460 Democrats were subdivided randomly into 10 districts, Republicans would probably be elected in six or more districts. However, if malevolent Democrats could draw district lines with precision, they might be able to isolate 100 Republicans in one district and win all the other district elections by a margin of one or two votes, thus capturing 90% of the state legislature while commanding only 46% of the popular vote."[42]

Justice Stevens clearly assumed that political groups and racial groups were equally cohesive and that partisans, regardless of how they were aggregated at the district level, would always vote for their affiliated party. Neither Stevens nor the Court ever stopped to inquire, however, into the nature of partisanship and how it varied. Stevens assumed a high degree of group cohesion and a consistency of individual voting behavior grounded in a strong partisan affiliation and attempted to set forth criteria for group definition. Yet, upon closer inspection, his criteria suggest that virtually any aggregation of individuals—under the right circumstances—could be regarded as a politically relevant group and would, therefore, be entitled to the consideration that had been denied them by Justice White in *Whitcomb* (152). Plaintiffs, said Justice Stevens, must show that

> they are members of an identifiable political group whose voting strength has been diluted. They must first prove that they belong to a politically salient class . . . one whose geographical distribution is sufficiently ascertainable that it could have been taken into account in drawing district boundaries. Second, they must prove that in the relevant district or districts or in the State as a whole, their proportionate voting influence has been adversely affected by the challenged scheme. Third, plaintiffs must make a prima facie showing that raises a rebuttable presumption of discrimination. (*Karcher*, 754–55, citations omitted)

This argument sounds similar to Dixon's description of groups in his condemnation of the simplistic one person, one vote standard.[43] It also embodies and amplifies the flaws that make Dixon's formula impracticable in the political process.

First, one must ask what is the difference between an identifiable group and a nonidentifiable one. The mere fact, for example, that a black minority is concentrated into a given area or district (as in *Whitcomb*) does not imply that the remaining white numerical majority functions as a cohesive political unit. It may be the case that racial cleavages dominate a particular municipality's or district's politics; but such a local cleavage might be subsumed at other electoral levels by broader cleavages (for example, the urban-rural cleavage), thereby causing the racially polarized district to vote as a bloc on certain issues.

Second, we must ask how to define and delimit a particular group and its salience. If a group can "disappear" sometimes (as the ghetto might have in the above scenario), how salient can it be? What makes it salient to begin with? One might argue that census data provide information regarding which groups exist at what electoral levels. But then again, one might argue, as Justice White did in *Gaffney*, that the census is little more than "an event" that provides a split-second snapshot that freezes otherwise fluid and dynamic social divisions (*Gaffney*, 746).

From a census one can determine, among other things, gender, race, and levels of income and education. These statistics all suggest group divisions, but are they all politically salient, identifiable, or exclusive? Furthermore, do they form the basis for a cohesive voting bloc? In *Gomillion* and *Whitcomb*, blacks and whites were segregated and easily identified; conversely, the demographics of an area such as Los Angeles, where blacks are concentrated in a few inner-city areas and Hispanics and white are dispersed, discourage easy group identification. Such overlapping of groups indicates the difficulty of administering to all socially relevant groups. In some cases, such as *United Jewish Organizations of Williamsburg v. Carey,* in which the Court permitted the division of a Hasidic community in order to create black-majority districts, the Court has seemingly found it to be impossible.

Finally, how many salient groups can there be? There is no simple answer to this question. The Court's attempts to establish ground rules for identifying the salient groups in a particular situation have only complicated the districting process by oversimplifying the complex nature and interrelationship between individual and group voting behavior. In the multimember districting case, *Thornburg v. Gingles,* the Court sought to discern between more and less cohesive groups and to develop the concept of "racially polarized voting" (62) as a means of determining whether a multimember scheme actually does discriminate against a particular group. The white majority, said the Court, must vote as a "bloc" consistently enough to "usually" defeat the minority's "preferred candidate" (51). The problem with this method, as Justice Brennan conceded, is that "there is no simple doctrinal test for the existence of legally significant racial bloc voting" (58). He went on to explain that virtually anything can affect the voter's decision.

> Age, religion, income, and education seem most relevant to the voter; incumbency, campaign expenditures, name identification, and media use are pertinent to the candidate; and party affiliation could refer both to the voter and the candidate. . . . [For the Court's purposes] the legal concept of racially polarized voting incorporates neither causation nor intent. It means simply that *the race of voters correlates with the selection of a certain candidate or candidates;* that is, it refers to the situation where *different races (or minority language groups) vote in blocs for different candidates.* (62, emphasis added)

Despite the fact that the Court cannot establish a manageable standard of measuring the interaction among and cohesiveness within political groups, it adjudicates such claims by invoking this simplistic formula for determining the existence of racial bloc voting, which focuses merely on correlations. "It is the *difference* between the choices made by blacks and whites—not the reason for that difference—that results in blacks having less opportunity than whites to elect their preferred representatives" (63).

If, as Brennan says, bloc voting is not necessarily evident, how can we be sure that mere correlations will indicate an actual denial of representational opportunity for black voters? (55–59). Furthermore, how would such reasoning apply to other groups, such as political parties, or to situations, such as the one described in Los Angeles, where more than one minority group is involved in an election?

Even if, as the Court asserted in *Thornburg* and as Justice Stevens maintained in *Karcher,* manageable standards could be established for the balancing and measurement of group representation and impact, the Court would still face the formidable task of establishing a consistent and manageable standard for defining and discerning "salient" political groups. Not every aggregation of individuals can be considered a bona fide political group (see, for example, *United Jewish Organizations of Williamsburg v. Carey*). So, regardless of the theoretical manageability of the Court's standard of fairness in representation, it serves no purpose if the groups to be measured are amorphous.

In order to prove that there is a separable, identifiable black interest that is not being represented, the Court must first show that there are voters who, in voting to express that black interest, form a cohesive black voting group—not just the existence of a group of blacks (see *Thornburg*, 51, 56). If black voters do not support the candidate who, as designated by the black group's leadership, is the preferred candidate, then there obviously exists disagreement about who the preferred candidate really is. Thus, the nature of a group, as well as the issues and candidates with which it is confronted, may make a difference in determining its behavior.

Davis v. Bandemer: The Widening Rift in the Court

In *Davis v. Bandemer*, Justice White changed his views as expressed in *Whitcomb v. Chavis* and asserted that the nature of a group—political or racial—makes no difference in its entitlement to representational opportunity and proportionality (125). Effectively, Justice White shifted the focus of debate from one of group definition to one of judicial capacity to fashion standards of representational fairness. As noted above, White asserted that the Court's fairness standard was manageable and applicable to all politically relevant groups, as defined by the criteria set forth by Justice Stevens in *Karcher v. Daggett* (*Karcher*, 760–61). In her concurrence in *Davis*, Justice O'Connor asserted that the fairness standard, regardless of its measurability, could not be used to adjudicate political gerrymandering claims, because political groups were too variable in their nature and composition to be measured (*Davis*, 155–57).

In some ways, one might argue, this developing rift in the Court is beneficial, because it indicates that the justices are finally addressing questions that at least touch upon some of the underlying issues of group representation: the difference among groups and the variability of individual partisanship. On the other hand, it seems that the Court is quickly approaching an impasse. In addressing the variability of group behavior, the Court will soon come to realize that in a single-member district system many groups simply will not be represented by name in the legislature. Dixon's vicarious representation framework notwithstanding, the problem of gauging the relative impact of subgroups within the larger parties in order to determine who, exactly, is losing out still requires resolution.[44]

As one solution to the problems of adjudication, the Court could concede that, as a judicial body, it lacks the capacity to establish a consistent, workable doctrine of group representational fairness. Were a system of proportional representation implemented, the Court would have less cause to enter this political fray.

Whether or not the Court is likely to recommend such a transition is debatable. The Court does not suggest that in a single-member system group representation requires proportionality: A "group's electoral power is not unconstitutionally diminished by the simple fact of an apportionment scheme that makes winning elections more difficult, and a failure of proportional representation alone does not constitute impermissible discrimination under the Equal Protection Clause" (*Davis*, 132, citing *Mobile v. Bolden*, 111, n. 7, Marshall, J., dissenting). The *Davis* plurality's lingering confusion is clearly evident here. If a failure of proportional representation does not violate the equal protection clause, and if it is permissible for a given electoral system to disadvantage an identifiable group of voters, how can gerrymandering be justiciable? This obvious confusion notwithstanding, methodological problems also persist.

Justice White pointed out that one election alone could not provide satisfactory evidence that a group's voting power had been diluted (*Davis*, 135). But this only begs the question: How many elections *would* serve as a satisfactory base for such a claim? What is certain is that so long as single-member districts are used with plurality systems of elections, minorities and losing parties will continue to be underrepresented.

Perspective: The Problems Underlying the Court's Problems

The inconsistencies in the attempts to establish a coherent and consistent judicial doctrine of representational fairness reflect similar inconsistencies in political science. Neither the Court nor political science has been able to formulate a means by which the gap between individual and group voting behavior might be bridged. Accordingly, attempts to do so by the Court, without the benefit of political science research (which has thus far not produced any coherent theory of group voting behavior), fall far short of their goal of creating a manageable and usable standard of fair group representation.

In addition, the courts and political science must also address differences in the behavior of divers types of political groups. Black voters will always retain their racial status, regardless of the particular election in which they vote, or the tensions within their political environment, or the district in which they reside; but voters of all colors change their partisan behavior frequently. Logic would dictate, then, that partisan and racial gerrymandering claims cannot be addressed in the same manner. Consider, for example, Justice White's assertion in *Davis*, where he explains how the "political profile" of a state can be defined.

"The political profile of a State, its party registration, and voting records are available precinct by precinct, ward by ward. . . . It requires no special genius to recognize the political consequences of drawing a district line along one street rather than another. It is not only obvious, but absolutely unavoidable, that the location and shape of districts may well determine the political complexion of the area" (128).

This is a sweeping statement, laden with assumptions about the availability and quality of electoral data—especially at the ward and precinct level, where units of aggregation may vary radically from decade to decade or even year to year. Further, it assumes that once such data could be assembled their implications for an area's political profile would be obvious. Which data are more indicative: registration data or electoral returns? When one considers that statewide voter registration data were not even kept by some states until the 1970s, it would seem that use of such data would be of little help in developing a profile. In fact, some states (Virginia and Hawaii, for example) do not maintain partisan registration records. Moreover, what would the profile tell us? As noted earlier, the increasing occurrence of ticket splitting and the shortening of presidential coattails indicate that partisanship is a variable entity. If a district votes Democratic at one level and Republican at another, what is its profile?

More importantly—and pertinently—what happens to that partisan profile when the area, or a part of it, is redistricted? Some or all of the voters will now make different choices among different issues and candidates. The nature of these new choices will naturally vary with the nature of the redistricting. Were voters moved across state legislative or congressional districts, or both? If they were moved only across state legislative districts, their congressional, as well as gubernatorial and senatorial, choices will not have changed. But it might be the case that the new choices made at one level of the electorate might change those made at another. For example, overrepresented Hispanic voter X is moved from a state legislative district with X's favorite incumbent Republican to the neighboring district in which two popular Democratic moderates are vying for a seat soon to be vacated by a similarly moderate incumbent Democrat. Citizen X votes for one of these two new Democrats, but because X still resides in the same congressional district, incumbent Republican congressman Y continues to receive voter X's vote.

If this scenario occurred as a result of a court-ordered attempt to negate the effects of a state legislative gerrymander, the Court would have failed in its mission, because voter X broke ranks and voted for the Democrats in the new district. Nonetheless, throughout the Court's opinions (as well as much of the political science literature on the subject), there is a pervasive assumption that if 100 Democrats are moved from district A to district B, they will all continue to vote as Democrats, regardless of the new electoral choices with which they may be faced. Such an approach to individual voting behavior does not account for much of the literature that indicates that previous partisanship is not necessarily determinative of future electoral decisions. It seems to assume that all groups of voters act as cohesively as the blacks involved in cases such as *Gomillion v. Lightfoot* and *Thornburg v. Gingles*.

The Court's model is built upon incomplete and inconsistent appraisals of the voting behavior of individuals and groups. The result is a process of analysis and implementation of districting plans that are grounded in faulty assumptions and provide no means by which the effects of these plans may be predicted or measured. If voters change their partisanship when redistricted, how can the effects of a districting plan be measured or anticipated?[45] The effects of redistricting on individual voting behavior have not been measured or predicted, principally because of the inability, thus far, of political science to resolve several questions regarding voting behavior.

The Political Science Model
of Voting Behavior and Its
Importance for Redistricting Analysis

Because redistricting and gerrymandering concern representation, any discussion of them must address the state of political science research, particularly its bearing on our perception of the relationship between voters and their elected representatives. Does political science analysis of elections support or challenge the notion that voters can be grouped according to their political behavior? Can constituencies be ascribed certain partisan profiles, as Justice White suggested in *Davis v. Bandemer?*

Whether and how much partisan electoral results tell us about the electorate's partisan divisions are especially important aspects of this inquiry. If partisan electoral results tell us little about the electorate's underlying partisan sentiments, then a partisan profile of a constituency based on votes cannot be used to determine whether vote dilution (and therefore, denial of representational opportunity) has occurred. Votes in this case might simply be choices among available options, unrelated to the ideological sentiments of the voters.[1] Under these conditions, a party could not claim that its voters were somehow dependent on the party for representation of their interests and policy preferences.

Partisan votes and partisan sentiments are, obviously, related in some way. However, the nature and extent of the relationship are unclear, because a vote for a party's candidate can be an expression of support for the party's ideology, an endorsement of the candidate, both, or neither. The vote may be an assertion of ideological support for a candidate who is a veritable totem of the party's ideological stands. It may be an assertion of support for the party's ideals despite the poor quality of its nominee, or it may be an endorsement of an attractive candidate, party affiliation notwithstanding. Finally, the vote for party A might be only a protest vote against party B.

To assess the validity of a partisan gerrymander claim, we must draw upon political science research to determine which interpretation of the vote's meaning is most feasible. A gerrymander claim is an assertion that the relationship between a party and the voters who depend upon it for representation of their opinions and the pursuit of their interests has been broken. The validity of the claim depends, however, on the validity of several assumptions about voting behavior and partisanship, which are still matters for debate. Most important is the assumption that voters vote in large part on the basis of ideological predilections that establish enduring ties to one party or the other—candidate quality notwithstanding. A corollary to this assumption is that all votes for candidates bearing the same party label are equatable qua expressions of support for and affiliations with that party.

Whether or not such staunch party loyalty exists and whether or not it translates into and can be inferred from partisan votes remain matters for some debate. There is little evidence to suggest that voters support a party regardless of the nominee's quality. There is, however, evidence of a strong, resilient predilection to support a particular party, which manifests in the voters' electoral behavior, unless the issues or the candidates in a given election repel the voters from their preferred party's choice. The more resilient the partisan attachment, the stronger the argument that the partisan vote reflects the underlying partisan profile of the electorate. The less resilient the attachment, the harder it is to claim that voters, by voting for a party's candidates, profess their partisan support and dependence on the party and the candidates for representation of the voters' ideological preferences.

It may therefore be the case that not all partisan votes are indicative of a close relationship between the voters and the party. If so, then grouping voters on the basis of the partisan votes may be no more relevant to determining a constituency's partisan profile than grouping them on the basis of eye color. Of course, no one would contend that green-eyed and blue-eyed factions were politically relevant to the determination of public policy. Even if we were to discover a high correlation between eye color and party vote, the least skeptical critic would be hard-pressed to contend that the relationship was not spurious. Though blue eyes may be a widely recognized trait, it is hardly a motivating factor in political decisions or a source of politically relevant solidarity among similarly eyed persons. Being a member of a racial or ethnic minority of course is likely to form the basis of such group cohesion. We must determine, then, where one's party identification or previous partisan electoral behavior fits on the continuum between eye color and race or ethnicity.

Clearly, the actual political relevance of a given group must be a function of the members' fidelity to the group. Whereas the potential relevance of redheads might be quite significant numerically, their actual political relevance is minuscule. Racial minorities, however, have transformed their potential relevance into very real political influence. Thus, recognizing a shared trait is not tantamount to realizing the political relevance of a group qua a political group; the determinative factor is the nature of the binding ties. Some group memberships, race for example, are immutable, while others, such as political party memberships, are quite flexible. But group membership—

immutable or not—does not necessarily dictate individual behavior, and coincidental individual voting behavior does not necessarily indicate the existence of shared partisan ties.

The Supreme Court's approach to gerrymandering has operated on the apparently reasonable assumption that *party vote* signifies *partisan affiliation* and that this relationship is sufficiently resilient to permit analysts to group voters into partisan blocs on the basis of their electoral behavior. Accordingly, the Court views the electorate as being composed of divers blocs of voters who can be assembled and reassembled in ways that can help or harm the electoral prospects of political groups. This view, however, is only partially sustained by political science. Although some studies, such as *The American Voter*, observe that there are enduring partisan predilections, others challenge the extent to which these predilections actually translate meaningfully into electoral results from which we can accurately take the pulse of the electorate.[2] The rise and fall of groups such as Democrats for Reagan, the Dixiecrats and Hoovercrats, and various third-party movements such as the Populists, the Progressives, and the American Independent Party demonstrate the inconstancy of partisan affiliation and loyalty. Furthermore, the phenomenon of ticket splitting indicates that partisan behavior (and therefore, the composition of partisan voting blocs) is not consistent even within a single election.[3]

The theory of realignment and critical elections first set forth by V. O. Key was grounded on a perception of the electorate similar to that espoused by the *Davis v. Bandemer* plurality.[4] Key's observation that *sometimes, some* elections display characteristics that indicate a marked break with previous voting patterns, producing a radically different and enduring realignment of voting blocs, engendered a heated debate about the rationality and sophistication of the American vote and the interpretability of election results. Were voters good, sophisticated citizens who took time to ponder issues and the parties' stands on them, or were they mere automatons whose voting behavior was based on inherited partisan ties or, worse, sheer ignorance?

Although the debate focused on the voter's mind, it reflected directly upon the relationship between the voters and the elected officials. If voters could be regarded as loyal supporters of one party or the other, then it could be argued that gerrymandering, or any other assault on the strength of a given party, was an assault as well on the representational opportunities of the voters affiliated with the injured party. If voters made their electoral choices only as a result of thoughtful consideration of issues, then it could not be argued that voters were wedded to one party or the other. Therefore, it could not be argued that gerrymandering, qua the ravaging of incumbents by diluting pockets of partisan support, actually harmed either the allegedly victimized party or the voters who were dependent upon that party for representation. In any given electoral decision, voters would base their choices on the issues of the particular election and then choose the party most likely to implement their desired policies.

One side of the debate about voter sophistication asserts the primacy of the voter's partisan predilections, or party identification, as the basis of voting decisions. This partisan predilection colors the voter's outlook on issues at stake during elections and seems to strengthen over time. The other side asserts that partisanship is contextually based. If voters' environments change, so too will their votes, because partisanship is not simply a habitual preference. *The American Voter,* which takes the former position, asserts that "in the period of our studies the influence of party identification on attitudes toward the perceived elements of politics has been far more important than the influence of these attitudes on party identification itself."[5] The contextualist approach asserts the opposite. At any given time, partisanship is derived from the factors that create a given political environment *and* the cumulative effect of similar factors in previous environments. Reconciling the two approaches is vital to redistricting analysis, especially when gerrymandering claims are involved, in order to clarify the evidence regarding the relationship between the parties-in-the-electorate and the parties-in-the-government.

Theories of Realignment and Critical Elections

In his seminal article, "A Theory of Critical Elections," Key made the following observation:

> Even the most fleeting inspection of American elections suggests the existence of a category of elections in which voters are, at least from impressionistic evidence, unusually deeply concerned, in which the extent of electoral involvement is relatively quite high, and in which the decisive results of the voting reveal a sharp alteration of the pre-existing cleavage within the electorate. Moreover, and perhaps this is the truly differentiating characteristic of this sort of election, the realignment made manifest in the voting in such elections seems to persist for several succeeding elections. All these characteristics cumulate to the conception of an election type in which the depth and intensity of electoral involvement are high, in which more or less profound readjustments occur in the relations of power within the community, and in which new and durable electoral groupings are formed.[6]

This passage describes electoral change that occurs in an almost catastrophic manner. During especially critical times, elections may be of a character that suddenly upsets an otherwise stable balance of political power. As well, it depicts an electorate composed of voters bound together by partisan ties into blocs that, when joined with other blocs, form the principal cleavages within the electorate.

Yet four years later, Key set forth several strong warnings to those who might formulate broad theories of partisan change based on his previous observations and hypotheses. Election returns, he noted, merely record periodic readings of the relative magnitudes of streams of attitudes that are undergoing steady expansion or contraction. Some elections may be "critical" in that they involve far wider movements and more durable shifts than do other elections. Yet, the rise and fall of parties may to some degree be the consequence of trends that perhaps persist over decades and elections may mark only steps in a more or less continuous creation of new loyalties and decay of old. The slow rate at which that process may occur suggests the potency of the frictions to change built into the electorate by its attachment to old symbols, old leaders, old parties. Only events with widespread and powerful impact or issues touching deep emotions produce abrupt changes. On the other hand, other processes operate inexorably, and almost imperceptibly, election after election, to form new party alignments and to build new party groupings.[7]

This passage suggests that the realignment that may appear to occur in a given election could, in fact, have occurred the day after the previous election or over several years in a gradual manner that could by no means be deemed critical. In addition, it suggests that electoral blocs are not as cohesive and durable as described earlier and that, due to voters' joining and quitting, they take on different shapes and sizes over time.

Key thus painted radically different pictures of electoral change and the nature of partisan affiliation. One suggests a scenario in which periodic earthquakes upset the electoral landscape; the other describes the change as constant and gradual. More important, the two scenarios question the reliability of employing electoral data for redistricting analysis. Since elections present a split-second snapshot of a dynamic electorate, how are we able to place the meaning of such a snapshot in the appropriate context? Key notes that "the ideal data for the purpose would consist of political life histories, extending over several generations, of random samples of population categories" (199). Thus, what appear to be two consecutive landslide elections could, theoretically, be separated by the precipitous fall and rapid recovery of a candidate's or party's approval ratings or by the decimation and reconstruction of a majority coalition.

It follows also that some elections, although they bring critical or realigning results, may not in fact represent fundamental shifts in the electoral power bases or the partisan leanings of voters. An uneventful election may keep voters away from the polls; similarly, a mundane candidate might quell any enthusiasm among his constituents. Apparent landslides can thus occur when popular interest is low. Despite the fact that such a scenario does not meet all of Key's criteria for a critical election, the outcome would have no less impact upon the composition of a legislature: if a party wins 100 percent of the seats in a legislature in an election with 20 percent turnout, its control is no less absolute than if it won with 80 percent participation. Its mandate might be subject to question, but its rule would be no less absolute.

Electoral change, even of critical proportions, does not therefore necessarily reflect the true underlying state of individual partisanship. And because individuals are the source of secular change, we must concern ourselves with the causes and nature of individual partisan shifts in order to gain insights into the accuracy of viewing the electorate as comprising cohesive voting blocs. Key noted that secular realignment involves the simultaneous processes of group homogenization and group dissolution. "Put baldly," he said, "the thesis might be, place a person of specified characteristics in a specified status in the social system and he forthwith becomes a Democrat (or a Republican)."[8] However, the speed and repetition of this process necessarily vary according to the individual voter and the political context in which the observations are made.

Party Identification and the Concept of Realignment

The American Voter observed that voters maintain a psychological attachment to one of the parties, an attachment similar to a religious affiliation. Warren Miller regarded the party as defining "the proper relationship between the person and the group-relevant components of social life."[9] It follows then that the party and its elite members are political cue givers to whom the identifier will turn in order to make a political choice. This identification, like religious affiliation, is the product of political socialization. You get it from your parents, and it tends to strengthen over time. It weakens or changes only during times of political upheaval or crisis.[10] During such circumstances the political system undergoes critical and realigning elections.

The nature of party identification and its determinacy in the voter's electoral choice remain matters for debate. On the one hand, proponents of its usefulness as a measure of the electorate's sentiments argue that it correlates highly with partisan vote—candidates notwithstanding.

> For virtually any collection of states, counties, wards, precincts or other political units one may care to examine, the correlation of the party division of the vote in successive elections is likely to be high. Often a change of candidates and a broad alteration in the nature of the issues disturb very little the relative partisanship of a set of electoral units, which suggests that great numbers of voters have party attachments which persist through time. . . . These loyalties establish a basic division of electoral strength within which the competition of particular campaigns takes place.[11]

But in any given election, voters may choose not to follow their partisan identification and cross party lines. To explain this, the authors of *The American Voter* use a "funnel of causality" metaphor to explain the process whereby the voter reaches an election day decision (24). In making such a decision, voters are first affected by partisan identification, which is their psychological tie to one of the parties and generally colors their political opinions. As election day approaches, voters weigh and consider the various short-term political factors that are germane to the particular election. Weighing these considerations in a manner biased by party identification, they vote for the candidate of one of the parties. Despite the rather frequent occurrence of electoral infidelity, the underlying partisan predilection of the electorate remains intact. "What is important to the current argument is not the shifting of the vote itself, but the fact that large-scale, and essentially unidirectional defections occur while the participants continue to think of themselves as adherents to the original party."[12]

This model begs the questions regarding the meaning and significance of electoral outcomes and partisan change. If, as it seems, the vote can be contrary to partisan identification, then which factor are we to use in determining the meaning of electoral change? *Party identification* is the psychological—almost instinctive—attachment to a particular group. *The vote,* on the other hand is the result of the process whereby voters reconsider and weigh their partisan predilections against the various policy statements made by candidates and parties in a given election.

This question bears heavily upon the determination of redistricting policies and theories of group representation. If the vote (which tends to fluctuate over time) contradicts party identification data (which are relatively consistent over time), how are we to decide which is the better or more appropriate indicator of the electorate's composition and the strengths of the various subgroups of which it is composed? When, and on what basis, can we be certain that a particular election or series of elections reflects the true partisan divisions of the society? Without a means of making such determinations, political scientists seem unable to define and identify existing electoral cleavages. Redistricters would thus be hard-pressed to draw districts that favored or disfavored a given group unless its members were numerous and consistent enough in their partisan behavior to guarantee a consistent bloc vote for the group's candidates. Accordingly, a classification is needed of both electoral changes and the environments in which such changes occur.

The American Voter's authors adopt and expand Key's classification of elections as a means of ordering the various types of electoral outcomes. To Key's special category of realigning elections, they add two more: maintaining and deviating. The former denotes an election "in which the pattern of partisan attachments prevailing in the preceding period persists and is the primary influence on forces governing the vote"[13] In a deviating election, "the basic division of partisan loyalties is not seriously disturbed, but the attitude forces on the vote are such as to bring about the defeat of the majority party." It is thus "a temporary reversal that occurs during a period when one or the other party holds a clear advantage in the long-term preferences of the electorate" (532–33).[14] This broader system of classification brings order to the discussion of electoral outcomes, but it passes little judgment on the voters themselves. How are they to be classified—by their psychological preferences or by their electoral behavior?

The original verdict of *The American Voter* is that there are few grounds upon which the two measures can be differentiated. The data suggest that in the 1950s voters relied overwhelmingly on their partisan identifications as a basis for their election day decisions. Little salience was given to the issues at stake in the particular election, and in fact, voters displayed a generally low knowledge of pertinent electoral issues to begin with. *The American Voter* sets forth four classes of voters, based on their respective levels of conceptualization. The first, A, includes respondents whose political evaluations had "any suggestion of the abstract conception one would associate with ideology"; B comprises persons who focused on short-term group interests; C refers to those who based their evaluations on their perceptions of the goodness of the times; and D is reserved for voters who made no allusions to political issues (222). They find that some 46 percent of their survey had little or no grasp of salient political issues and that party identification was the principal determinant of the vote.

Given these findings, the sophistication of voters becomes an issue for debate and, furthermore, the derivability of the meaning (if one existed) of a particular election is similarly subject to question. If voters rely, for the most part, upon instinctual or habitual affiliations such as party identification, how can we draw conclusions about the state of the electorate (or the apparent changes within it) from voting returns? Not only were voters seemingly uninformed; their assimilation of the myriad bits of political information, says Philip Converse, also followed no pattern of logic.

[The] unfamiliarity of broader and more abstract ideological frames of reference among the less sophisticated is more than a problem in mere articulation. Parallel to ignorance and confusion over these ideological dimensions among the less informed is a general decline in constraint among specific belief elements that such dimensions help to organize. It cannot therefore be claimed that the mass public shares ideological patterns of belief with relevant elites at a specific level any more than it shares the abstract conceptual frames of reference.[15]

Bearing this in mind, Converse maintains that if most of the electorate was as unsophisticated as the data indicated, the content and meaning of electoral change was highly questionable.

Since the resurgence of the Republicans in the Eisenhower period depended primarily upon crossing of party lines by people who normally considered themselves Democrats, we were able to isolate these people to see from what levels of conceptualization they had been recruited. We found that such key defections had occurred among Democrats in the two bottom levels at a rate very significantly greater than the comparable rate in the group-interest or more ideological levels. In other words, the stirrings in the mass electorate that had led to a change in administration and in "ruling ideology" were primarily the handiwork of the very people for whom assumptions of any liberal-conservative dimensions of judgment were most far-fetched. (218)

It should be noted, however, that this verdict is concededly timebound. Observers such as Converse are not making the blanket conclusion that voters were, for the most part, inherently stupid, irrational, or unsophisticated. What they *are* saying, according to Warren Miller, is that the voters, although not necessarily inherently so, were *acting as if they were* unsophisticated in this particular study. Nor was it the case that reliance upon or adherence to party identification for the voting decision was, in and of itself, an inherently unsophisticated or irrational act.

> The argument has never been made that the historic origins of party identification are free of policy connotation and reflect only presumed moral or aesthetic qualities inherent in one party or the other. The transmission of a sense of party identification has never been assumed to be antithetical to the coincident transmission of other symbols giving political content to the meaning of party identification. The content is indeed often of a primitive and unsophisticated kind, but it is of the kind that permits an economic recession in 1974 to evoke old feelings that "our" Democratic party is the party of the common man and will defend those of us in the working class while "their" Republican party is the party of big business and the upper classes. No matter how limited the content, there has never been any assumption that somehow party identification and party voting must be irrational and at odds with policy-oriented behavior.[16]

But if this is the case, what can be inferred from electoral change? The propositions of the party identification model as set forth by the authors of *The American Voter* do not leave us with a coherent set of parameters for interpreting elections. Party identification is a product of a socialization process that does not necessarily involve conscious rational decisions in the process of establishing one's partisan affiliation; and party identification does endure and strengthen over time unless a crisis occurs that is strong enough to uproot it. Accordingly, there appears to exist a long-term stability in the electorate due to the infrequency of such crises.

Nonetheless, short-term defections from one's party identification are likely to occur as a result of the issues and party platforms in a given election, while the underlying affiliation remains intact. The likelihood of such defections is inversely related to the strength of the partisan identification. In the event that the crisis is strong enough, massive, permanent defections may occur, thereby resulting in partisan realignments. Thus, despite the occurrence of partisan realignments, we still may expect to observe short-term defections in voting behavior, which are caused by the voter's reconsideration of his vote vis-à-vis his or her party identification as a result of a particular election's tone.

This train of thought leaves us with a somewhat bleak outlook for interpreting the meaning of elections. Elites, who are most informed about issues, seem most likely to defect in a given election, because their knowledge provides them with reasons to reconsider their party identification. Those in the lower categories who by virtue of their lack of sophistication seem to be most likely to refer to party identification cues, should be the least likely to switch. But, the authors found that just the opposite was the case—the least sophisticated voters were the ones who were moving the most.[17]

Accordingly, political science finds itself in a quandary regarding the interpretability of election results. Party identification is not a reliable basis for electoral interpretation because it is not necessarily a rational or determinative factor in the voter's electoral choice. On the other hand, election results (and especially changes in electoral behavior) seem to be composed for the most part of votes cast in strict adherence to party identification or votes cast by voters who are uninformed or breaking away from their partisan sentiments. For partisan change to be meaningful, it has to be placed in a rational context. Key sought to establish such a context in his response to *The American Voter*.

Key's Response and the Definition of Voter Sophistication

In *The Responsible Electorate*, Key argues that voter rationality—and therefore, voter choice—must be analyzed with regard to the political context in which voters make their decisions.[18] He maintains that "voters are not fools" and that the quality of choices they make when voting is dependent upon the quality of the options presented by the parties and candidates. He differentiates among three types of voters: "standpatters" (who voted in two consecutive elections for the same party's presidential candidate), "switchers" (who changed their party vote) and "new voters" (who either were too young to or did not vote in the last election). He concludes that voters who switched were not as unsophisticated or uninformed as Converse suggests.

In fact, he finds that switchers switched because they agreed more with the issue positions of the opposing party's candidate. Key contends that his findings do not establish that party switchers differ materially in level of interest from the standpatters. But, he notes, the character and level of information of the average switcher varied in response to the changing political topography of different election contests (19–28). Thus, the voters who switched in an extremely polarized election were likely to be different from those who switched in a relatively placid one. Despite the higher regard he held for switchers, Key maintains, ultimately, that *The American Voter*'s model of voting still held (90–103, 141–48). The pattern of the data, he writes, "probably confirms the significance of Angus Campbell's model built on party identification. Standpatters stay by the party even though they agree with the opposition party. But those who agree with their party are most inclined to stay with it. Policy preference reinforces party loyalty. Those whose party preference conflicts with their party voting record are most likely to defect" (150).

He disagrees, however, about how to interpret the variability of partisan behavior that occurs despite the endurance of party identification. Voters, he says, are not necessarily preoccupied with politics. When they do turn their attention to voting, though, they can be expected to react only as rationally and thoughtfully as the quality and clarity of the campaign propaganda permits. "Engulfed by a campaign fallout composed chiefly of fluffy and foggy political stimuli, the voter tends to let himself be guided by underlying and durable identifications, group loyalties, and preferences rather than by the meaningless and fuzzy buzz of the transient moment" (113–14).

By suggesting that voting behavior can be affected by the political environment (as defined and conditioned by the parties, candidates, and propaganda), Key not only defends the voter against charges of ignorance, irrationality, and irresponsibility but also asserts that the electoral environment in which campaigns are conducted can not be regarded as a constant. To the extent that this environment is dynamic, its impact on voters *has* to be taken into account, because electoral choices in one environment are not necessarily equatable with those in another, despite the fact that the choice of party labels and individual party attachments remains the same over time.

Key contends that what the authors of *The American Voter* may have regarded as irrational or irresponsible electoral behavior can not only be excused (because of the parties' poor performance in framing issues) but can also be regarded as quite reasonable—even responsible—since the quality and sophistication of the voters' behavior is a response to the quality of campaign propaganda. Converse disagrees: he argues that attributing the apparent absence of thought exhibited by the voters to the lack of clarity with which political cues are transmitted does not prove that voters are any more rational or thoughtful. Instead, it proves only that they are responsive to stimuli. Key, says Converse, "prepares the reader deftly for proof that the electorate is a more *responsive* one along issue lines than others have supposed, and some interesting evidence is then supplied. But a responsive electorate need not be a responsible one, or notably rational, as [*The Responsible Electorate*'s] titles suggest."[19]

Although Key and Converse focus their arguments on whether voters can be regarded as thoughtful, rational participants in the electoral process, the ramifications of their dialogue extend much farther than simply passing a verdict on citizens. The basis for their disagreement has an important impact as well on the conclusions we are able to draw based on our interpretation of electoral outcomes. If voters are irrational actors who vote according to partisan predilections, regardless of the changing political circumstances in which different elections occur, then electoral outcomes that declare one party or the other the winner cannot necessarily be regarded as accurate indicators of informed political sentiments.

To the extent that votes are merely habitual expressions of an almost instinctual party identification, they tell us very little; they therefore provide a shaky basis upon which to interpret the meaning of electoral change. If voters are thoughtful and attentive to the changes in the dynamic electoral environment, then their votes under one set of circumstances for one of the two parties cannot necessarily be compared to or equated with votes under another set of circumstances. As the political environment changes, so too will voters' perceptions; they may still be forced to choose between only Republican and Democratic candidates, but the meaning of these partisan votes will change over time. Furthermore, the divergence of party vote from party identification challenges the notion that the vote can be regarded as an expression of *partisan* preference. Thus, the meaning of votes cast for the two parties will certainly change, despite the nominal constancy in the choice of parties (Democrats and Republicans) on election day. A Democratic vote in a given year is not equatable to one in another year unless it can be argued that the circumstances in which the two contests occur are virtually identical.

Burnham's Entry into the Debate

In "Theory and Voting Research," Walter Dean Burnham addresses this issue by moving beyond the question of voter sophistication and focusing instead on the impact that the acknowledgment of the relationship between environmental change and the meaning of voting behavior has had on political science's ability to interpret and predict electoral outcomes.[20] If voters behave differently when the political environment changes, how can events from qualitatively different electoral eras be compared on the same continuum— endurance of the two-party system notwithstanding?

Burnham asserts, for example, that, since the political and social environments of the nineteenth and twentieth centuries were so different, it is difficult, if not impossible, to compare them on the same scale, despite their nominal similarities. Noting, for example, the drastic changes that occurred between the nineteenth and twentieth centuries in rates of turnout,[21] demographics, governmental structure, party organization, and so on,[22] he maintains that "the circumstantial evidence suggests very strongly, to my view, that elections meant something very different to 19th-century Americans than they mean to their descendants today; that parties also meant something quite different."[23] Burnham asserts that survey research is timebound and maintains that longitudinal studies of electoral change lack explanatory power if they fail to account for changes in the political environment in which a given set of observations occur.

He explains that if, as Key stated, the quality and meaning of electoral behavior are conditioned by the nature of the political era, then measures of the partisan change over time are of questionable value. Periods of intense partisan activity and high voter interest cannot be compared to their opposites if the extent and nature of the changes that brought about such shifts in partisan activity are not taken into account. "Let us make the assumption that when politics matters, when it is not a spectator sport but is widely perceived to raise life-and-death issues, people behave as though it matters. In other words, let us assume that a significantly larger fraction of the electorate will be politically active and relatively politically aware in crisis situations than surveys of contemporary American presidential elections would lead us to believe, and that the deeper the crisis, the more politicized the electorate."[24] Burnham's assertions were confirmed when his call for a replication of *The American Voter* was answered by Nie, Verba, and Petrocik's *The Changing American Voter*.[25]

Nie, Verba, and Petrocik find that the "sophistication" of voters is a function not only of the political environment at any given time but also of the nature of that environment at the time of one's first voting experience. Accordingly, voters who began voting in the rather placid 1950s are more likely to rely on party affiliations than to weigh and consider issues charging the political agenda, because the latter were less characteristic of politics in the 1950s. Similarly, those who first voted in the 1960s think more along issue and ideology lines as a result of the political turbulence of the decade brought about by the civil rights movement and the Vietnam War. Despite the apparent differences in political awareness evidenced in surveys, voters were probably no more or no less sophisticated in the 1960s and 1970s than they were in the earlier era. The process by which party identification is instilled is likely to vary, ironically, with the nature of the times during which the voter entered the electorate. The public, to no one's surprise, changes its views regarding different issues as the times and political conditions change (345–56). More important, Nie, Verba, and Petrocik find additional changes in the "structures and belief systems" of voters. Not only do the opinions of voters change, so also does the way in which such opinions are formed.

Furthermore, *The Changing American Voter* shows that what appears to be partisan change in the aggregate may in fact be voter replacement—a phenomenon that, the authors argue, played a significant role in the New Deal realignment. During the 1920s, a large pool of new potential voters was created as a result of immigration, extension of the franchise to women, and the coming of age of the children of the immigrants who had arrived at the turn of the century. Since none of these groups of new voters had an electoral history, so to speak, or parents with an electoral history that had been influenced in turn by their parents and so forth, they felt no compulsion to adhere to any established patterns of partisan identification and quickly fell in step with the Smith campaign's ethnic appeal in 1928 and then the New Deal in 1932 (ibid.). Hence the New Deal realignment was due to *voter* change as well as *partisan* change.

Burnham also notes that such "replacement" groups are catalysts of realignment, because critical elections occur "only when enough time has passed so that for the vast majority of voters the 'heroic age' of the preceding major cleavage has receded into the historical past."[26] Since they had not voted, they had no memories of past "heroic ages." Thus, in addition to the necessity of a crisis as a condition for realignment, the voters must be of such a partisan persuasion that they are likely to overcome any partisan influences that they may have received from their parents.

Accordingly, Burnham and *The Changing American Voter* indicate that aggregate electoral data can be deceiving. Massive demographic change can alter a constituency's partisan profile, even in the absence of political crisis. Similarly, a constituency's profile may appear to be constant, despite significant demographic changes that do not show up in aggregate electoral data. Such findings substantiate Burnham's arguments that there are significant qualitative differences between political eras. These differences arise not only from Key's secular realignments but also from forces militating against the transmission of party identification across generations, such as voter replacement and changes in the political environment. Alluding to the changes that occurred during the 1960s and 1970s, Burnham explains: "These and other well-known manifestations of generational rupture in political consciousness during this era [1964–76] presuppose processes which, taken together, add up to 'political desocialization.' That is, they are processes out of which *failure* to transmit values across generational lines becomes a dominant analytical problem."[27]

Thus, political desocialization suggests not only that different generations may view parties and politics differently but also that the nature of politics and individual political reasoning may change to such an extent that contrasts can more reasonably be assumed than qualitative similarities among birth cohorts. As Burnham notes, "the basic point is that the classics of the survey-research literature on political attitudes and voting behavior were grounded on the implicit assumption that macro-systemic variables were essentially (or could for all practical purposes be regarded as) constants in the United States. The evidence presented by *The Changing American Voter* makes it clear that they are indeed variables."[28] This being the case, fluctuations in the strength and nature of partisan identification suggest that the nature of the political groups, whose existence is a function of partisan ties, would also undergo changes. Logic thus dictates that if shared partisan ties fluctuate, so too must the nature, cohesiveness, and therefore, political relevance of the groups with which partisans identify.

Redistricting Analysis and the Problems of Electoral Interpretation

This debate among political scientists about the interpretability of election results makes accusations of gerrymander based on partisan redistricting analysis that much more questionable. The difference of opinion between Key and the authors of *The American Voter* indicates that the logic of equating party vote and underlying partisan sentiment is debatable. Burnham's discussion contends that a party vote in a given year is not necessarily equatable with a vote for the same party in any other year. Together, these observations require a reexamination of the representational relationship between voters and the parties and an investigation of the impact of redistricting qua an alteration of macrosystemic parameters on partisan voting patterns. The variability of these parameters undermines the logic of the Court's approach to voting and group behavior, as well as its approach to redistricting.

The redrawing of district lines is, in some cases, tantamount to changing the electoral environment of the affected voters. Furthermore, its immediate impact is similar to the electoral replacement described in *The Changing American Voter;* it brings new voters into a preexisting polity and thereby sows the seeds of political change. To the extent that these hypotheses are true, redistricting will, in and of itself, inject an increased element of unpredictability into the electoral behavior of the affected voters and thus decrease the likelihood that they will retain previous patterns of partisan behavior. Even if the affected constituencies show no change in their partisan behavior, we cannot determine whether this was due to (1) the strong partisan ties on the part of the voters, (2) the similarity of the candidates and issues in the old and new districts, or (3) a low level of sophistication and interest on the part of the affected voters.

The implication of this hypothesis is that partisan gerrymandering—or affirmative remedial gerrymandering—may in fact be self-defeating. If changing the electoral environment causes changes in partisan behavior, the Courts can no longer rely on data from previous elections or the assumption of group cohesion as bases for its redistricting decisions.[29] The Court will now need to predict the impact of the redistricting on prior partisan patterns in order to determine whether the affected voters were denied some representational opportunity that existed in their previous district.

The durability of partisan patterns (and the validity of the assumption that such durability implies consistency of partisan sentiment) is a key component of gerrymandering analysis. The sine qua non of a valid partisan gerrymandering claim is the proof by the plaintiff party that there exist pockets of staunch partisan supporters who, for whatever reason—low levels of sophistication or extremely strong ideological ties to the party—have retained their strong support for the party despite being redistricted into a district in which their votes are wasted, thereby diluting the plaintiff party's support. If such constant partisan behavior is not evident, the gerrymandering claim is subject to challenge, because the apparently loyal partisans changed their voting patterns when they were shifted into a new district. Establishing our ability to apply a partisan label to a given constituency is the first step in any analysis of the impact of redistricting. If affected constituencies do not maintain at least a modicum of partisan consistency, then one party or the other cannot claim the constituency as part of its partisan base. Therefore the plaintiff cannot claim that it has been gerrymandered.

The behavior of constituencies in districts held by strong incumbents provides an analogous situation. The security and power of incumbents is well documented.[30] In some cases, they are strong enough to discourage political challengers and draw voters across party lines. As a result, the entrenchment of incumbents may produce noncompetitive voting patterns in an otherwise competitive district. Incumbent retirement may therefore result in an apparently drastic alteration of a district's voting patterns. An opposition party that is demoralized by a strong incumbent's presence is more likely to support a candidate, and thereby encourage opposition voters to turn out, once the incumbent is gone. As well, the incumbent's retirement may generate enhanced interest and primary competition within his own party.[31] The resulting competitive (or at least *more* competitive) election may appear to be as critical a change in voting patterns as any portrayed by the realignment literature; however, the observed changes would tell us little about alterations in the underlying partisan cleavages in the district, since the changes would be due partially to the change in the election day candidate choices.

Like redistricting, incumbent retirement changes the cast of characters on election day. Shifting a town from one district to another serves the same purpose as an incumbent's retirement: it changes the political environment by substituting variables (new candidates and new issues) for constants (incumbents or previously familiar candidates and issues germane to the old district). If significant alterations of the district's partisan patterns were to occur in the wake of the incumbent's retirement, we would infer that the apparently overwhelming support for the incumbent's party had as much to do with the incumbent's power or personality as it did with party affiliation. Increased knowledge of individual voting habits and how they change will be helpful in determining the extent to which changes wrought by the redrawing of district lines affect individual fidelity to divers political groups (that is, partisanship). Once this is known, the courts will be in a better position to remedy the injuries visited upon groups by unfair redistricting processes.

To determine the effect of environmental changes and redistricting, we must ascertain and define the profile of a town as well as particular political circumstances. What is its partisan balance and turnout level? How constant are these over time? Then we must categorize the environmental changes themselves. Was the constituency moved across state legislative or congressional districts, or both? Did an incumbent retire? Was a given election actually contested?

We might expect that the nature of the redistricting shift and the profile of a town would dictate the change in the town's partisan behavior and that the most extreme shifts (for example, moving a competitive town with a rather low turnout rate from the district of a strong Democratic incumbent to the district of a similarly strong Republican) would create the most noticeable partisan changes in electoral behavior. Similarly, we would expect shifts between similar districts to produce minor changes.

A more complex example would involve a town that always votes heavily for its Democratic state senator but leans toward the Republicans in other respects. We would be wary of moving this town in order to make the heavily Republican senatorial district next door more competitive. Since the state senate vote appears to be an aberration (a popular incumbent, perhaps?), we could predict that, absent a similarly popular Democratic challenger in the new district, this town would vote Republican.

Redistricting analysis cannot operate on the assumption that partisan profiles of affected constituencies are constant or accurate indicators of partisan sentiments. The fact that redistricting itself alters some of the parameters of the voting decision requires that we work instead from the assumption that existing partisan profiles are, indeed, variables.

4

Theories and Methods
of Gerrymandering Analysis

A redistricting plan can be assessed from the point of view of either the incumbent legislators or the voters who are to be represented. Much of the literature that focuses on the fates of legislators assumes that the behavior of the party-in-the-electorate is consistent, that individual voters maintain a consistent propensity to vote for one party or the other, and that the party label is more important to the voter than the nature of the candidate who wears it.[1] Such assumptions, if valid, permit the analyst to focus strictly on issues such as the translation of party votes into party seats in the legislature and to pass judgment on the inherent fairness of a given districting scheme by determining whether or not the scheme in any way disadvantages the voters of one party or the other. However, since the partisan propensity of any individual voter or group of voters is not necessarily consistent from one election to the next, decisions about the fairness of a districting scheme cannot be made simply by using prior election results to predict a redistricting plan's impact or by comparing a party's percentage of the overall vote to the number of legislators bearing that party's label who hold seats after a given election.

In a district system of representation, the party-in-the-government has as many faces as there are legislative districts; similarly, the party-in-the-electorate is actually several *sub*parties-in-the-electorate, each of which votes for a different face of the party-in-the-government. Although elected officials do wear party labels, we cannot in turn assume that party affiliation is the key determinant of partisan voting in the electorate.[2] Thus it is not necessarily valid to argue that partisan voters have somehow been denied their "fair and effective representation" simply because the party-in-the-government controls a percentage of legislative seats that differs from its overall percentage of the vote.

Any assessment of the fairness of a districting scheme must also take into consideration institutional factors such as ballot form, the parties competing for votes, and the system of voting. For example, the voter's choice is limited by the number of parties on the ballot. In the United States the plurality system of voting makes it virtually impossible for third parties to gain or maintain any enduring political strength. The growing number of independent voters, however, suggests a certain dissatisfaction with the two major parties; yet, with the exception of local third parties such as those in New York, Hawaii, and Puerto Rico, independent voters are limited in their election day options to the two major parties. Thus to speak of fair representation of the two major parties in the legislature overlooks clear indications that the two major parties do not necessarily represent all of the electorate's political tendencies and that their percentages of the vote are influenced by the system of voting and ballot form as well as by partisan ties to the voters.

Since the impact of any system of voting on representation is conditioned by the way voters actually vote, redistricting analysis must include a focus on the behavior of the party-in-the-electorate. Without a clear understanding of the electorate's voting patterns, any attempt to determine whether a districting scheme fails to represent accurately the "true" partisan divisions within the electorate or biases the translation of votes into legislative seats will be inaccurate or uninformed.

Current Methods of Gerrymandering Analysis

Many formulas and measures have been proposed as means to detect and remedy a gerrymander. These fall into two broad categories: geographic and results-oriented. The former focus on knowing a gerrymander when we see one; the latter set forth measures by which gerrymanders can be identified, even when we cannot see them cartographically.[3] Inevitably, the conclusions drawn from either measure depend upon the spatial distribution of voters within and across constituencies.[4] A gerrymander requires different methods to dilute the voting power of a geographically concentrated bloc on the one hand and a more dispersed one on the other.

The different between racial and partisan gerrymandering is a good example. Racial gerrymandering involves group conflicts that are not necessarily between political parties; in fact, not a few of the racial gerrymandering cases occurred either in urban areas or in the old South, where the conflict erupted within the Democratic party. In such cases, the cohesiveness of the contending voting blocs is hardly subject to question, due to the racial polarization and geographic concentration of the constituencies involved.[5] Partisan gerrymandering, on the other hand, deals with blocs of voters who may be spread unevenly across an entire state and who may be less loyal to the party that is making a gerrymandering claim than they are to a particular incumbent who happens to bear that party's label. This being the case, we must ask how far from the cohesiveness of racially polarized blocs may the parties-in-the-electorate stray before we question their own cohesiveness and therefore the standing of the party-in-the-government to cry gerrymander in the first place?

Analysis of partisan gerrymandering thus requires establishment of a reliable, broad-scale measure of partisan behavior that uses criteria such as voting data and registration figures, which may be less clearly interpretable than data from more compact or racially polarized areas. This task requires more than simply reading a legislative district map, tracking electoral results, or establishing a partisan profile based on some "normal" vote measure. It requires the incorporation of measures of consistency in aggregate electoral behavior, in light of the changing conditions under which the behavior occurs.

For example, denial of fair representational opportunity could more easily be determined in a constituency that maintained a consistent turnout level and partisan split than in one whose partisan behavior and turnout vary from year to year. Changes may occur in a district that cause sympathetic changes in the partisan behavior of its voters; an incumbent may retire, a scandal may erupt, or a president's coattails might lengthen momentarily and upset an incumbent. Some areas will behave more consistently than others, despite the fact that the circumstances in which elections are held may be changing. In the same way, some constituencies can be expected to respond more than others to changes wrought by redistricting. Before we address claims of gerrymander by legislators we must examine the behavior of the voters (upon whose representation such claims are based) and determine the extent to which the parties-in-the-electorate may have been redefined or altered in their size by a change of districts.

Standard Criteria for Assessing Gerrymandering

Gerrymandering analysis ultimately focuses on the various conceptions of fair representation and the extent to which a given districting scheme produces a fair result. The effects of such a scheme can be assessed on the basis of several criteria: (1) geographic concerns such as district compactness and maintaining competitive districts; (2) measurements of the fairness of the electoral result produced by a given districting scheme or electoral system; (3) its impact on minority party incumbents; and (4) its perceived impact on voting blocs in the electorate.

Bernard Grofman sets forth twelve prima facie indicators of gerrymandering, which serve as a quick index of the geographic criteria. He places "particular reliance" upon four: (1) differential treatment of incumbents, (2) use of concentration and dispersion (of partisan groups) techniques, (3) deviations from compactness and violation of existing political boundaries, and (4) minimization of competitive districts. These criteria apply in varying degrees to the effects of gerrymandering on the party-in-the-electorate and on the party-in-the-government, noted above. Differential treatment of incumbents addresses the fate of legislators and the battles that occur within the party-in-the-government. The other three focus upon the voters themselves and their spatial distribution.

Incumbents and their fates actually pose an intriguing problem for gerrymandering analysts: should they be protected and, if so, to what extent? If voters actually do vote for parties rather than candidates and are consistent in their propensity to vote for particular parties, then the sacking of minority party incumbents by forcing them to run against each other in redrawn legislative districts is certainly tantamount to the denial of representation to the minority party's voters.[6] If the opposite is true—if voters vote for candidates rather than parties—then the ravaging of incumbents can be regarded as an egregious denial of representation only insofar as the choice between one pair of candidates provides more of an opportunity to be represented than the choice between another pair. Thus, although the retention of incumbents (or at least their fair treatment by the party that controls the redistricting process) appears to be a key point of contention in gerrymandering, it is not necessarily consistent with the other criteria set forth by Grofman.

In light of the strengths of incumbents and their ability to attract votes across party lines, stressing the importance of creating and maintaining competitive districts seems contradictory to the goal of fair representation.[7] Since incumbents exercise such power on election day, the attempt to maintain even concentrations of partisans within districts seems futile. The desire to prevent the unfair dispersion or concentration of partisans in the electorate seems futile as well, since incumbents are able to appeal successfully to voters outside their own party. An incumbent is likely to become eventually entrenched and virtually unbeatable (especially at the congressional level) in his district. Accordingly, any desire to maintain even dispersions of partisans and to preserve competitive districts is at odds with any desire to protect—or at least treat fairly—incumbents.

This is not to argue that incumbents have some right to go unchallenged; the issue in gerrymandering disputes is whether the differential treatment of incumbents is justifiable. However, to argue (in the name of increased partisan competitiveness within districts) against the preservation of incumbencies or to argue in favor of measures that might weaken them also serves ultimately to undermine the rights of the voters themselves to elect and retain the representatives of their choice, regardless of the fact that those representatives may seldom be challenged.

Finally, stressing the importance of geographical compactness and the preservation of existing political boundaries also conflicts with the desire for competitive districts. Unless a state is characterized by an even distribution of partisans, the desire to maintain compactness will certainly lead to uneven partisan divisions within districts and, therefore, the inability to realize the goal of competitiveness. If partisans actually were distributed evenly across a state, the goal of competitiveness could still be unattainable. Unless there were equal numbers of partisans statewide, the larger party would be guaranteed a majority in each district; it could win in every district with as little as 50 percent plus one vote. Thus, such a system would be absolutely unrepresentative, yet each district would be extremely competitive.

Competitiveness is a protean concept; competition at the electoral level does not necessarily result in competitiveness in the legislative process. Thus, for redistricting, it is not an especially helpful measure of fairness. In addition, criteria such as Grofman's clearly presume the existence of a special relationship between the voter and incumbent. The denial of the opportunity to vote for the same candidate that one voted for previously can be regarded as suspect only if we assume that the redistricted constituency and its voters would be represented less effectively by the new district's candidates. If voters perceive a given candidate or party as the ideal personification of their partisan values, then any redistricted voter should feel as cheated when forced to choose among candidates in a new district as a gerrymandered voter would feel when forced to choose between two candidates from the same party in a collapsed district. In the first case, the quality of representation would be diminished; in the second, the quantity.

Whereas geographic criteria focus on the physical aspects of the electorate, results-oriented criteria address voting behavior and seek generally to establish some base measure of partisanship for a state and use it to determine the extent to which election results under a given redistricting plan deviate from its ideal. The two most common such measures are the employment of a base-race, or composite vote, measure and the use of a seats-votes or swing ratio.[8]

The base-race method, says Charles Backstrom, entails the selection of an "adequate indicator of relative strength of the political parties in the state's electorate."[9] The indicator is usually a composite or average of several races that occur within a state or some obscure, "invisible," yet typical race, such as that for state public service commissioner, which, "can be considered a relatively accurate measure of base partisan electoral strength, because, in the absence of an extensive personality-oriented campaign, voters tend to follow only the cue of party designation on the ballot."[10]

The assumptions underlying this approach overlook several key factors that affect elections generally. The existence of a popular incumbent or a personality-oriented campaign at some electoral level other than public service commissioner might encourage a voter to vote a straight party ticket. On the other hand, personalities of candidates notwithstanding, Backstrom's view fails to account for phenomena such as "ballot-fatigue" and "roll-off."[11] Since only the most motivated voters are likely to make it all the way down the ballot to public service commissioner, the use of such "invisible" races would probably skew the resulting measure of the state's true partisan divisions in the direction of the party with the larger number of strong or highly motivated partisans. Furthermore, any use of such invisible statewide races, which are purportedly insulated from candidate- or district-oriented factors at other electoral levels, clearly presumes that to be Democrat or Republican means the same thing in one constituency or at one electoral level as in another, regardless of the attractiveness of particular candidates or the strength of incumbents or party organizations. The frequent occurrence of ticket splitting undermines this argument.

Thus the assumption that some insulated base race can be employed as an accurate measure of a state's true partisan division ignores the possibility that representation of voters may be a function of the appeal of particular candidates as well as party affiliation. It overlooks the important impact that incumbency may actually have on the partisan behavior of a district. Such measures may represent an "ideal" partisan breakdown, but since legislative districts do not conform to any ideal conditions, these measures would certainly be inappropriate.

The seats-votes and swing ratios are inappropriate for similar reasons. In their most basic form, they are both measures of the disproportionality of representation in a particular districting system. The employment of both measures begins with the assumptions that, in an ideally fair electoral system, X percent of the vote would translate into X percent of the legislative seats and that a Y percent increase in a party's proportion of the vote would deliver a similar increase in its share of the seats. To the extent that the first assumption does not hold, a system is considered unfair; if the second does not hold, it is said to be biased.[12]

Several problems plague the use of these measures. First and foremost, they assume that the state itself can be regarded as a cohesive political unit and that, therefore, measures of partisan fairness can be derived by aggregating the partisan votes from the various legislative or congressional districts into a statewide partisan profile. Second, they consequently ignore district-specific considerations such as incumbency, whether or not an election is contested, and other regional factors that might predispose a district to favor one party more than the state average would indicate.[13] Finally, and as a result, such measures assume that, for all intents and purposes, a Democratic vote in one district is comparable to (and, therefore, equatable with) Democratic votes in other districts, regardless of the candidates for whom the votes are cast.

Although more recent analyses have begun to address such district-specific considerations, they still overlook the problem of equating votes cast under different conditions.[14] Votes cast for candidates wearing the same party label in different districts are not necessarily equatable. Intuitively, we would expect strongly Republican constituencies to remain so from one election to the next. However, in reality we find the strongly Republican constituencies can rapidly turn into strongly Democratic ones (and vice versa) if given the opportunity. Such changes can occur as a result of an incumbent's retirement, the advent of a challenger, an increase in turnout, or redistricting. Finally, the seats-votes approach assumes that party affiliation is the principal determinant of the voter's decision. This derives from the previously noted assumption that votes for different candidates wearing the same party label are comparable. Theories of voting behavior do not, however, substantiate this assumption.

If voters are dyed in the wool partisans, or if they are at least consistent in their propensity to vote for a certain party, then the concept of a partisan profile can be useful because, like a normal vote measure, it provides an index of a constituency's actual partisanship. But this presupposes that partisan behavior is consistent in the first place. Partisan behavior is no doubt conditioned to some extent by who the candidates are. A popular incumbent is likely to maintain high partisan support and draw votes from across party lines and may even discourage challengers from competing. An unpopular incumbent would be less likely to do so. In either case, there are reasons to expect a high abstention rate when the incumbent is unchallenged. If the popular incumbent is unchallenged, turnout might be low because the election's result was regarded as a foregone conclusion. In the case of an unpopular incumbent, voters might prefer abstention to casting a vote for an incumbent who retains office simply because there are no credible challengers. This suggests that turnout and partisan vote can very significantly in response to changes in the cast of characters on election day. Even in successive contested elections, the competitiveness of the election will certainly be affected by the candidates' personalities as well as the voters' partisan propensities.

Redistricting can cause significant changes in affected constituencies that result in the alteration of their previous voting patterns. When moved, redistricted constituencies face different candidates, perhaps different party organizations, and different political environments composed of different towns and cities. We would expect the partisan profile of the redistricted constituencies to change as a function of their partisan propensities as well as in response to the changes that resulted from the redrawing of districts. The less fixed the partisan preferences of the redistricted constituencies were, the more likely they will change once they are moved.

Our assessment of the impact of redistricting on the representation of an affected constituency's interests—fluidity or consistency of voter preferences notwithstanding—is a function of how we regard the purpose of elections and the theory of representation to which we subscribe. Do voters vote to choose the best candidate for the job (partisanship notwithstanding), or do they vote to elect a representative body that closely mirrors their partisan preferences? On what basis are the voters' votes cast?

The Meaning of Votes

How we interpret the meaning and significance of a vote bears heavily on the legitimacy of a gerrymander claim. If, for example, we regard votes as random choices among candidates, there is no basis upon which to argue that the votes have any meaning regarding policy or partisan preferences. Under these conditions, gerrymandering is not an issue.

If, on the other hand, we regard all votes for a party as espousals of partisan preference or loyalty, then it is a fairly easy task to determine a group's size and fair representation by counting its votes and comparing them to the number of seats its members hold in a legislature. In a district system of representation, however, voters can be said to vote for candidates as well as parties. The question therefore arises, to what extent can a vote be regarded as (1) a partisan preference independent of candidates, (2) a candidate preference independent of party, or (3) a combination of candidate and partisan preferences?

If voters vote strictly on the basis of who the candidates are, then it is impossible to determine a constituency's partisan divisions, because the votes are not cast as statements of partisan support. Since no two candidates are identical, a constituency's partisan divisions are likely to change somewhat when parties designate new candidates. If this is the case, we must consider whether votes for different candidates bearing the same party label are comparable.

The *candidate voter* can support candidate A for any number of nonpartisan reasons; thus a vote for A may actually have nothing to do with A's party affiliation. If this is so, we cannot regard the result of an election between A and B as necessarily a referendum on partisan ideals. The contest may indicate only that A is more popular than B in this particular constituency. Candidate voters are thus difficult to categorize as partisans, and their votes do not provide us with any basis for determining whether particular constituencies within a district have been denied their fair representational opportunity. The observed divisions within the district simply indicate a preference between two particular candidates; if two new candidates run in the next election, there would be no basis upon which to compare the results unless it could be argued that the candidates were virtually identical. Elections in different districts are similarly incomparable.

A voter's decision is doubtless influenced by both partisan and candidate issues, and the impact of either will vary in response to the particular election day political conditions. Accordingly, voters' partisan preferences are unlikely to be consistent; thus, fair partisan representation is quite difficult to determine or measure when we are dealing with candidate voters. Partisan gerrymanders therefore seem to be harder to perpetrate or detect than many analysts argue. A claim of the denial of representational opportunity presupposes the existence of identifiable partisan groups of measurable size and representation. But if group membership (as defined by votes) varies in response to candidate changes, then we must determine the extent to which candidate and party are separable in the minds of the voters before deciding whether a redistricting scheme is actually a gerrymander.

Current Analysis of Electoral Systems

Whether or not a particular electoral system is unfairly biased against a given political group is the subject of much writing about gerrymandering and representation. The debate about the fairness of a given electoral system ultimately boils down to a choice between some form of proportional representation and the single-member majority or plurality system. However, the impact of an electoral system on fair representation depends as well upon how we view the behavior of the party-in-the-electorate and its relation to the party-in-the-government.

If voter preferences are fixed, and if the purpose of elections is only to create a legislature that will represent all the political tendencies in a state, then proportional representation appears to be the only means of ensuring fair treatment of all political groups. Any other system would certainly militate against at least one group's fair representation. Single-member districts would ensure that the losing party in each district is underrepresented, unless we had faith in some form of virtual representation, which contends that the interests of partisan minorities in one district are protected by their party's representatives in other districts. As a result, gerrymandering would pose a grave threat to fair representation in a single-member district system where voters had fixed partisan preferences. On the other hand, if voter preferences are fluid, then the SMP system of voting would pose a threat only to the parties-in-the-government and their ability to maximize the number of votes they receive in a given election.

Where an electorate is characterized by fluid partisan preferences, the parties-in-the-government must run as many attractive candidates as possible, because they cannot depend on any sort of inherent partisan loyalty to motivate voters to support them. In a single-member system under such conditions, the parties would have to appeal to as many nonpartisan electorates as there are districts. Under these conditions, however, redistricting would pose a threat only insofar as it requires parties-in-the-government to maximize the attractiveness of their nominees. If voters vote only for the most attractive candidate (party affiliation notwithstanding), then they will be represented in any district by the candidate they vote for in a given election. Under these conditions, losing minorities can be said to be underrepresented only because more people found the other candidate more attractive. Of course, voters do not behave in such a nonpartisan manner; there is a better than fifty-fifty chance that a voter will choose a given party or candidate over another. But the chances that a voter will do so are also less than 100 percent. The threat of redistricting thus varies in relation to the likelihood that a voter will cast a consistently partisan (as opposed to candidate) vote.

In a proportional representation system in which the voters are characterized by fluid preferences, the onus once again is on the parties-in-the-government to run as many attractive candidates as possible. In systems of proportional representation, candidates with less than a plurality of the votes can still gain seats in the legislature for their party. However, if voters in this system vote for attractive candidates instead of party platforms, there will still be no impact on the partisan representation of popular interests, since the voters did not go to the polls to have their partisan interests represented in the first place.

This begs the question regarding the rights of political parties-in-the-government and the effects of gerrymandering and redistricting on their control of legislatures. The rights of the parties-in-the-government to control a certain number of seats must ultimately be grounded in the assertion that the parties actually do represent cohesive, identifiable constituencies of voters who feel a partisan tie to the parties-in-the-government and who depend upon one of these parties to ensure the protection of their interests. Any complaint about the biases inherent in an electoral system or the electoral system's failure to produce acceptable seats-votes outcomes must be substantiated by proof that the votes cast are somehow representative of a cohesive *partisan* constituency that is bound to the party by more than the general appeal of a particular candidate. Without such an electoral connection the minority parties-in-the-government have no grounds upon which to complain about mistreatment by their corresponding majority. The question remains then, how can we discern the nature of the connection between the party-in-the-government and the party-in-the-electorate?

Response to These Criteria

The standard criteria for redistricting analysis share several weaknesses. They assume that a candidate's party label is the determining factor in voting and that voter preferences are more or less fixed. They also presume a uniformity of voter interest and partisan propensity across elections in the same year and across years at the same electoral level. Similarly, they assume that conditions across the various legislative districts in a state are comparable. Finally, they set forth contradictory requirements for the preservation of electoral competitiveness while avoiding damage to the reelection prospects of incumbents.

Effective partisan gerrymandering (and any remedy for it) is thus likely to occur only under ideal political conditions. It would require an electorate characterized by consistent partisan divisions and composed of voters who are unlikely to cross party lines. Although such conditions would not permit us to account for changes in the behavior of individual voters, we would be able to estimate confidently the partisan profile of the constituencies. However, variation in turnout and the common occurrence of ticket splitting prevent us from operating under such ideal circumstances. If each year a town or a district splits along similar partisan lines and roughly the same numbers of people vote, then predicting an election result would require only the use of the previous election results. Depending on the political circumstances, however, it may in fact be unrealistic to expect any degree of consistency under even the most similar conditions from year to year.

Therefore, in order to determine the extent to which a gerrymander can be said to dilute unfairly the vote of partisans in a given area, we can compare patterns in the electoral behavior of unchanged towns with those of redistricted towns. This will permit us to compare normal fluctuations in partisan behavior with those induced by redistricting.

Where an incumbent is repeatedly returned to office, for example, the partisan division is virtually fixed and the constituency can therefore be deemed Democratic, Republican, strongly Democratic, and so on. But when conditions change, it may not be possible to designate only one partisan division for the constituency. Staunch partisans might vote for their party regardless of its candidate, while others might not be so loyal. Accordingly, we would expect to see changes in the propensity of a given constituency to vote a certain way, which correspond to the changes that occurred in its electoral environment as well as its previous partisan behavior.

Since changes can occur at any time and due to a variety of circumstances, we can compare changes that occur as a result of an incumbent's retirement or defeat with those that occur as a result of being moved from one district to another. In order then to determine whether partisan groups have been denied their fair representation, we must measure the extent to which the redistricted areas behave in a manner similar to other districts that underwent similar circumstantial changes, whether redistricted or not.

If for example, a group of towns, moved from a district held by a Democratic incumbent to one held by the Republicans, began to vote for the latter's incumbent, claims that those towns or the Democratic party had been gerrymandered would appear to be unfounded, since the towns altered their behavior in response to new election day choices. Claims of foul play would be no more justified than claims asserting that the party's loss of a district after retirement of an incumbent was somehow unfair.

One might argue that these Democratic towns and the Democratic party had nonetheless been gerrymandered because the moved towns had no option but to vote Republican in their new district, since the powerful Republican incumbent discouraged viable Democratic challengers. The moved towns, however, would retain the option of *not voting*. To argue that staunch Democrats would vote for the Republican incumbent (instead of abstaining) simply because he was there undermines our ability to apply meaningful partisan labels to constituencies and the utility of using electoral data to determine whether a gerrymander had been perpetrated in the first place. For all we know, these towns might have been Democratic in their previous district because there were no viable Republican challengers. Thus, in order to engage in gerrymandering analysis, we must begin with the assumption that votes can be taken at face value.

Absent redistricting, the case of a retiring incumbent is especially instructive for the purposes of this study. If the towns in the retired incumbent's district do not change their partisan behavior when the incumbent steps down, the district's partisan divisions were likely conditioned by the incumbent's party. However, if we observe a marked shift in voting *away from* the retired incumbent's party, we would argue the opposite. In the former case, the towns with consistent voting patterns would seem to be amenable to claims to gerrymandering, because they appear to comprise cohesive blocs of partisans. In the latter case, since voting behavior is more dependent upon the circumstances in which elections occur, so too would representation. Accordingly, the voters and the parties would be harder pressed to claim that they had been gerrymandered.

Gerrymandering analysis must address two general questions. First, under differing electoral circumstances, how different or consistent is the partisan behavior of towns? Second, under similar or consistent circumstances from year to year, how much shifting occurs? If partisan behavior and membership in parties-in-the-electoral fluctuate, the aspirations of gerrymanderers (or those who seek to foil them) may be self-defeating to some extent, because we cannot be sure that parties-in-the-electorate will act similarly from one election to the next. The assertions of political groups or parties who claim to suffer from partisan gerrymandering retain their merit only insofar as these groups can be identified in a consistent manner and can therefore be said to be *representable*. In the same way that the party of blue-eyed voters can make no claims of partisan gerrymandering or, more relevant to our purposes, the Progressive party or the American Independent party have no standing to challenge a redistricting scheme that favors only Democrats and Republicans, those who claim to represent the interests of the allegedly gerrymandered Republican or Democratic minority must be able to prove that the voters they lost in the last round of redistricting actually are loyal members of the afflicted party. If voters who voted Democrat in District A vote for the Republican candidate when moved to District B, the claims by the Democratic party of having their electoral power diluted are certainly subject to question.

If a group's existence is merely a function of particular circumstances, it cannot claim to be adversely affected simply because it disappears when redistricting causes circumstances to change. The strength of the party-in-the-electorate can be diluted as easily by a popular incumbent's retirement as by redistricting. With regard to the fortunes of the parties-in-the-government, viable claims of vote dilution seem to require proof not only that particular groups of voters were cohesively partisan in previous elections but also that, in postredistricting elections, those same voters continue to behave as group members by supporting the party-in-the-government, despite the fact that it is now represented by a different candidate. A finding that, from year to year, partisan behavior is consistent, regardless of the changes that may occur in candidate and district factors, would indicate that there are blocs of voters that at least appear to be cohesive and therefore susceptible to gerrymandering and partisan vote dilution. Such variability in voting behavior necessitates a method for identifying alleged gerrymanders that accounts for the regular variations occurring in partisan behavior as well as the factors that may cause changes in that variation.

Discussion of My Method

If a state's political groups or parties-in-the-electorate behave consistently year after year, we need to use only last year's data to predict this year's electoral outcome. Accounting for changes that occur due to population and demographic shifts as well as increases in turnout during presidential election years (and barring any sort of electoral upheaval or realignment), we would expect that from year to year partisan percentages would shift a bit but remain fairly easily predicted. The ideal prediction equation incorporating the possibility of partisan change for electoral data would then be

$$D\%t = \alpha + \beta 1 D\%(t - 1).$$

In this equation, $D\%t$ is the Democratic percentage of the vote in any given town in year t and $D\%(t - 1)$ is the percentage in the previous election year. The intercept, α, represents whatever pro- or anti-Democratic bias may exist statewide, and β—the slope—represents the propensity to vote Democratic from one election to the next.

Note that this equation does not describe the state's partisan divisions; it does not tell us that the state is "so Republican" or "so Democratic." Instead, it describes the changes in the state's partisan behavior occurring from one year to the next across all of its towns. Accordingly, it lets us predict the Democratic percentage of the vote for any given town in a state, based on the behavior of the state as a whole—that is, as an aggregation of all its towns. Thus, the equation describes the partisan behavior of the state as the sum of the partisan behavior of its parts. However, this equation will not necessarily provide a comprehensive description of the state's partisanship. If, for example, one or more of the state's congressional or legislative districts has been dominated by a popular Democratic incumbent who is seldom challenged, we might question not only the strength of what would appear to be overwhelming partisan ties to the Democratic party but also the implications of such an equation, which measures statewide, partisan changes. The extensively documented advantage of incumbency suggests that the apparent partisan loyalty, as registered in partisan vote totals, might well be merely a function of the incumbent's popularity or name-recognition advantage. In cases of one-party hegemony we must therefore be skeptical of any appearance of consistent partisan behavior by voters. The fact that voters routinely pull the lever next to the dominant party's or strong incumbent's name says nothing about how voters might act were they given a choice between two equally attractive candidates of different parties.

Doubtless, the success of a long-standing incumbent might have effects on the partisan leanings of the district's electorate. If the incumbent is seldom challenged because the other party believes that he or she is unbeatable, the voters might become nominal members of the incumbent's party, only because their election day choices offer them no other possibilities. If the incumbent were to retire, the party out of power might be willing to present a challenger for the seat, since there would be no incumbent's name-recognition advantage with which to contend. Under such circumstances, voters who previously had been offered only one choice on election day would now be faced with a choice of candidates from both parties. Notwithstanding the voters' tendency to identify with the party of the erstwhile incumbent, we would expect a certain shift of the vote totals to the party out of power.

If we assume that incumbency and a district's political tradition are significant determinants of voting behavior, then we must assume further that any change that occurs in these two factors will be reflected to some extent in a corresponding change in the behavior of the district's voters. Thus, we need to account for these incumbent and district characteristics. A more complete general prediction equation would then read

$$D\%t = \alpha + (\beta 1 + \beta 1 DIST)D\%(t - 1) + \beta 2 DEM + \beta 3 INCD + \beta 4 INCR,$$

where $D\%t$ is the Democratic percentage of the vote in year t; α is the pro- or anti-Democratic bias; β is the propensity to vote Democratic; $D\%(t - 1)$ is the Democratic percentage of the vote in year $(t - 1)$; $DIST$ is a dummy variable accounting for the impact of party and incumbency control of a given district on the propensity to vote Democratic ($1 =$ Democrat, $0 =$ Republican); DEM is an intercept dummy variable accounting for any pro- or anti-Democratic bias that may result from party control of the district ($1 =$ Democrat, $0 =$ Republican); $INCD$ is an intercept variable accounting for any pro- or anti-Democratic bias that may result from whether a Democratic incumbent runs ($1 =$ yes, $0 =$ no); and $INCR$ is an intercept variable accounting for any pro- or anti-Democratic bias that may result from whether a Republican incumbent runs ($1 =$ yes, $0 =$ no).

By adding such additional variables to account for district-specific political conditions, we address the possibility that such factors actually affect the outcome of a particular election and, correspondingly, the partisan profile of a town or district. We might expect, for example, to see the Democratic vote strengthen in towns where the Democratic incumbent was running for reelection. Similarly, we would expect to see a gradual erosion of the Democratic vote in districts where the Republican incumbent is strong.

The Choice of Data

The data I use were drawn from Democratic election results for Congress, Governor, and State Senate in Connecticut and Massachusetts from 1972 through 1986.[15] Not all towns and cities of these states are included in the sample: 134 of Connecticut's 169 towns are included; 336 of Massachusetts' 350 towns are included. I was unable to acquire data on some of the omitted towns. Data for others were unavailable, as a result of poor bookkeeping or failure on the part of the states to preserve the integrity of the boundaries of wards and precincts. As a result, it was impossible to compare units of aggregation in these omitted towns over time. In some cases, for example, in a given year, Ward 1 might be a triangular district in the center of town; the next year, Ward 1 might be a dumbbell-shaped district in the northwest corner, and in the place of the old, triangular Ward 1 sits rectangular Ward 7. Such circumstances are problematic only in towns that were divided between legislative districts and where the division changed as a result of redistricting. The simultaneous alteration of the division, as well as the location and shape of wards and precincts, prevented the use of data from such towns. Problems such as these were not uncommon in Connecticut and in fact are common in many states. Before selecting Connecticut and Massachusetts, I surveyed the data from some thirty states. In many cases, municipalities are free to determine and change the boundaries of local units of vote aggregation. Since such units are frequently designed with the convenience of voters in mind, they are not necessarily drawn in the interests of political science.

I chose Massachusetts and Connecticut ultimately because of the relatively good quality of their data and their manageable size: the sample totals 470 towns. Furthermore, despite their strongly Democratic voting patterns, the two states provided interesting contrasts that lent themselves to my analysis. Connecticut underwent minor redistricting changes in 1982. It retained the same number of congressional districts (six), and the only redrawing of district lines was designed to balance populations. As a result, minor adjustments were made at the borders of districts. Massachusetts, on the other hand, experienced a much more drastic redistricting in 1982 because it lost a congressional seat. As a result, two incumbents were forced to run against each other in a much-publicized race, and one of the two Republican members of the congressional delegation was defeated.

Thus these two states, with their numerous small towns and their preservation of municipal boundaries, provided a large and useful sample of data. The units of data aggregation are towns; accordingly, changes that occurred within the towns (that is, the redrawing of ward and precinct boundaries) did not affect the comparability of election results over a period of time.

The States as Political Units

Analyses of gerrymandering frequently use a state's partisan split as a benchmark for measuring the fairness of a given redistricting scheme. The difference between the partisan division of a particular district and that of the state as a whole and the difference between a party's share of the statewide vote and its share of legislative seats serve to indicate the bias or unfairness inherent in a given redistricting map.

This chapter and the next examine the statewide partisan behavior of Connecticut and Massachusetts in order to determine the consistency of their partisan profiles. A certain amount of shifting in the states' profile from one year to the next can be expected, due to turnout changes, presidential elections, and similar factors. Nonetheless, gerrymandering analysis is predicated on the assumption that states and constituencies have consistent and measurable relative propensities to support candidates of a given party.[1] For example, constituencies where the majority of voters *register* as Republicans can be expected to *vote* Republican.

If this is so, then states or other aggregations of voters can be used as partisan benchmarks for gerrymandering analysis, and we can expect the state to maintain a consistent partisan profile. If, on the other hand, the state actually behaves merely as a geographical aggregation of independent regions, then its use as a measurement standard would be inappropriate.

The State's Partisan Profile

For a state, or any other political unit, to have a partisan profile, this profile must be reasonably consistent from one year to the next. That is, if 75 percent of a state's voters supported a Democratic candidate one year and 80 percent supported the Republican candidate for that same office in the next election, that state could not be designated as either Democratic or Republican. Similarly, if the state as a whole were divided 60 percent Democratic and 40 percent Republican in a series of gubernatorial elections, but the various political subdivisions changed their partisan profiles from one election to the next, we would again hesitate to say that the state had a distinct partisan profile. Even though the state might consistently support Democratic candidates with 60 percent of the vote, those candidates' support would not be consistently drawn from any particular part of the state.

In a gubernatorial contest, the consistency of the distribution of the partisan vote is less important to the outcome than the consistency of its cumulation. As long as one party gains a majority, it wins, regardless of where the votes come from. However, when we seek to analyze legislative elections and redistricting plans, the distribution of the partisan vote becomes more important than the aggregate results.

If we use gubernatorial data, we can say that a state is X percent Democratic or Y percent Republican simply by counting votes, because the state is, for all intents and purposes, one big constituency. All voters are presented with the same choice of candidates, and therefore, Democratic votes in one part of a state are comparable to those in another. Votes cast in legislative and congressional elections are not so comparable, however, because such elections involve numerous different slates of candidates, which are presented in the divers legislative districts. Accordingly, we cannot necessarily aggregate such data in order to label a state, because we cannot be sure that a Democratic vote in one district would be a Democratic vote in another: a voter in one district might not favor the Democratic candidate in the other district.

We must be cautious when employing any measure of partisan fairness that aggregates (and therefore, equates) votes from a state's divers legislative or congressional districts without accounting for their idiosyncracies. The residents of various districts participate in unique elections that entail choices among different, *district-specific* slates of candidates. Although candidates generally run under party labels, we cannot be certain whether votes are cast for candidates or for their designated parties.

If a state is merely a loose aggregation of election districts, vote totals from such distinct election districts do not necessarily reflect statewide preferences. We might just as easily aggregate several states' gubernatorial results in order to determine a regional partisan profile. A profile derived in this manner would be meaningless, because one state's popular governor might not be favored in the neighboring state, even though both governors bear the same party label. Any such statewide measure would also overlook the state's regional differences in partisanship. Two states may appear to be 60 percent Republican when we aggregate all votes cast in congressional elections. However, if one state is characterized by a sharp regional partisan division, while the other state's partisans are spread more uniformly across the state, the two statewide partisan measures will have radically different meanings.

Thus, to the extent that states behave as loose aggregations of independent polities that are defined by election districts, a *statewide* measure of partisan fairness cannot be applied to legislative or congressional districting plans.

The Consistency of Statewide Partisan Behavior

An analysis of voting behavior in Massachusetts and Connecticut demonstrates the unsuitability of statewide measures of partisanship. Although the two states are historically Democratic, they differ markedly in the party control of their elected offices, as well as in the strength of party organizations. In Connecticut, a competitive state, Republicans are a stronger factor, in terms of raw votes cast in elections to both the state senate and Congress, than in Massachusetts (tables 5.1 and 5.2). Despite the absence of a strong Democratic party organization such as that which has functioned in Connecticut for so long, the Democratic party has dominated Massachusetts politics.[2] As a result, during the period of this study, the state senatorial and congressional delegations were never less than 80 percent Democratic.

This dominance by Massachusetts Democrats has led to the frequent occurrence of unchallenged Democratic candidates in general elections at both legislative levels and the not infrequent occurrence of uncontested Republican state senatorial primaries. Third-party candidacies are more common and sometimes more successful in Massachusetts, where they garner as much as 5 percent of the congressional vote, than in Connecticut. Major party dominance has also led to the entrenchment of incumbents in Massachusetts. During the period of this study, not one incumbent at the congressional or state senatorial level lost a reelection bid, and the overwhelming majority of incumbents ran for reelection.[3]

The weakness of the Republican party vote in Massachusetts is especially remarkable when compared to the rate of voter abstentions.[4] As many as 15 percent of the ballots were left blank in congressional elections, and as many as 24 percent were left blank in state senate elections. The average Republican tallies of 24.6 percent in congressional elections and 19 percent in state senate elections indicate the extent to which Republican voters are either apathetic or nonexistent.

Registration data in both states are remarkably consistent from year to year. During the period of this study, Connecticut's electorate remained evenly divided among the Democrats, Republicans, and independents, while the Massachusetts split hovered around 45 percent Democrat, 15 percent Republican, and 40 percent independent. These figures, however, are *statewide* measures of registration; as a result, they tell us little about the behavior of the states' towns. If, for example, from one year to the next, one town experienced a surge in Republican registration of a thousand voters while another experienced a decline of equal size, the statewide registration figures would remain the same, despite the fact that a change had clearly occurred. More realistically, we might expect such changes to occur in many different towns and to varying degrees from one year to the next. Although the many changes at the town level might

Table 5.1 Connecticut Voter Data, 1972-1986

	1972	1974	1976	1978	1980	1982	1984	1986	average	standard deviation
Congress										
Number of Votes										
Democrat	657,265	620,029	681,730	592,396	680,186	577,340	667,668	544,938	627,694	48,523
Republican	690,838	440,207	651,250	423,474	640,157	485,491	761,647	433,977	565,880	125,836
Other	2,778	18,197	15,980	5,033	4,295	6,536	2,973	735		
Percent of Votes										
Democrat	48.7	57.5	50.5	58.0	51.4	53.9	46.6	55.6	52.8	3.88
Republican	51.1	40.8	48.3	41.5	48.3	45.4	53.2	44.3	46.6	4.12
Number of Seats										
Democrat	3	4	4	5	4	4	3	3	3.75	0.66
Republican	3	2	2	1	2	2	3	3	2.25	0.66
Percent of Seats										
Democrat	50	66	66	83	66	66	50	50	62.13	10.82
Republican	50	34	34	17	34	34	50	50	37.87	11.01

State Senate

Number of Votes

Democrat	611,186	617,491	691,638	562,110	666,008	598,891	625,779	531,931	613,129	48,142
Republican	725,130	442,414	648,036	444,606	651,147	453,765	738,096	415,730	564,865	129,468
Other	1,480	1,634	4,534	225	189	2,027	6,892	0		

Percent of Votes

Democrat	45.7	58.2	51.5	55.8	50.5	56.7	45.6	56.1	52.5	4.65
Republican	54.2	41.7	48.2	44.2	49.4	43.0	53.8	43.9	47.3	4.56

Number of Seats

Democrat	13	30	22	26	23	23	12	21	21.25	5.69
Republican	23	6	14	10	13	13	24	15	14.75	5.69

Percent of Seats

Democrat	36	83	61	72	64	64	33	58	59	15.83
Republican	64	17	39	28	36	36	66	42	41	15.63

Table 5.2 Massachusetts Voter Data, 1974-1986

Congress	1974	1976	1978	1980	1982	1984	1986	average	standard deviation
Number of Votes									
Democrat	1,168,252	1,509,521	1,249,311	1,420,832	1,300,334	1,618,131	1,198,143	1,352,074	156,308
Republican	401,300	723,119	471,755	757,828	586,315	719,755	250,385	558,637	177,595
Other	129,149	112,744	88,328	25,165	3,788	8,161	54,640	60,282	46,987
Blank	197,720	248,878	234,682	310,385	213,414	249,007	274,108	246,885	34,781
Total	1,896,421	2,594,262	2,044,076	2,514,210	2,103,851	2,595,054	1,777,276	2,217,879	319,019
Total D + R + O	1,698,701	2,345,384	1,809,394	2,203,825	1,890,437	2,346,047	1,503,168	1,970,994	307,211
Percent of Votes									
Democrat	61.60	58.19	61.12	56.51	61.81	62.35	67.41	61.28	0.03
Republican	21.16	27.87	23.08	30.14	27.87	27.74	14.09	24.65	0.05
Dem% D + R + O	68.77	64.36	69.05	64.45	68.78	68.97	79.71	69.15	0.05
Rep% D + R + O	23.62	30.83	26.07	34.39	31.01	30.68	16.66	27.61	0.06
Number of Seats									
Democrat	10	10	10	10	10	10	10	10	0
Republican	2	2	2	2	1	1	1	1.57	0.49
Percent of Seats									
Democrat	83.3	83.3	83.3	83.3	90.90	90.90	90.90	86.55	3.76
Republican	16.6	16.6	16.6	16.6	9.09	9.09	9.09	13.38	3.71

State Senate

Number of Votes

Democrat	1,059,376	1,565,173	1,271,558	1,515,981	1,291,026	1,541,995	1,007,074	1,321,740	212,741
Republican	374,121	479,285	391,194	401,602	418,718	494,211	376,772	419,415	44,981
Other	39,493	28,184	33,055	41,481	9,010	41,847	40,353	33,346	10,982
Blank	331,501	522,339	348,269	607,602	385,026	517,139	353,074	437,850	101,103
Total	1,804,491	2,594,981	2,044,076	2,566,666	2,103,780	2,595,192	1,777,273	2,212,351	341,061
Total D + R + O	1,472,990	2,072,642	1,695,807	1,959,064	1,718,754	2,078,053	1,424,199	1,774,501	250,147

Percent of Votes

Democrat	58.71	60.31	62.20	59.06	61.37	59.41	56.67	59.68	0.02
Republican	20.73	18.46	19.14	15.64	19.90	19.04	21.20	19.16	0.02
Dem% D + R + O	71.92	75.51	74.98	77.38	75.11	74.20	70.71	74.26	0.02
Rep% D + R + O	25.40	23.12	23.07	20.50	24.36	23.78	26.45	23.81	0.02

Number of Seats

Democrat	42	45	44	43	43	42	42	43	1.07
Republican	8	5	6	7	7	8	8	7	1.07

Percent of Seats

Democrat	84	90	88	86	86	84	84	86	2.14
Republican	16	10	12	14	14	16	16	14	2.14

Note: Data not available for 1972.

numerically cancel each other out, leaving the appearance that statewide registration levels had remained constant, the partisan profile of the state would in fact have undergone a significant change. How can we measure and account for such changes?

The Use of Regression Analysis

To measure and account for such change, the scope of analysis must be narrowed to follow the behavior of the state qua the sum of its parts—that is, its towns. If we were to conclude from the registration data that Connecticut's or Massachusetts's registration levels really had remained constant, we would need to assume that there had been no numerical canceling out of votes. By using regression analysis, we can determine whether or not this is the case. Using the prediction equation

$$D\%t = \alpha + \beta 1 D\%(t - 1),$$

described in the last chapter, we can measure the town-to-town consistency of a state's voting behavior from one election to the next. If the partisan registration levels remained the same for each town in two consecutive elections, the prediction equation for registration data would read

$$D\%t = 1 D\%(t - 1),$$

with R-square $= 1$.

The β of 1 in this case indicates a prediction that registration levels would remain the same. The R-square of 1 indicates that this prediction was error free: that is, for every town in the state, the predicted registration level at time t was accurate. If the entire state (that is, all the towns) were to experience a change in registration levels from one year to the next, the prediction equation would read

$$D\%t = \alpha + \beta 1 D\%(t - 1),$$

with $\alpha \neq 0$ or $\beta \neq 1$. Thus, if Democratic registration levels dropped five points from one year to the next, the equation would read

$$D\%t = -5 + 1 D\%(t - 1),$$

with R-square $= 1$. If there were a 10 percent increase in Democratic registration in every town, the equation would read

$$D\%t = 0 + 1.1 D\%(t - 1),$$

with R-square $= 1$.

Naturally, it is unlikely that every single town in a state will be characterized by the same partisan change; nonetheless, the regression equation will tell us the extent to which this is the case. For example, our prediction equation may read

$$D\%t = D\%(t - 1),$$

suggesting that there was no change in registration levels. However, the lower the value of R-square, the more error prone our equation will be. Thus, if our R-square is only 0.8, our prediction equation accounts for only 80 percent of the variance in predicting registration levels at time t. The lower R-square suggests that the state behaves more as a loose aggregation of independent and distinct polities than as a cohesive political unit. Consequently, a single prediction equation cannot adequately measure the voting behavior of all towns in a given state.

The prediction equations for registration data in both states indicate that virtually no change occurs in registration levels from one year to the next (see tables 5.1 and 5.2). The βs for both states' prediction equations are very close to 1, and the R-squares are all greater than 0.9. These data indicate not only that statewide registration levels are quite consistent from year to year but also that this consistency is reflected uniformly across the two states' towns. A good depiction of such statewide cohesion is shown in figure 5.1, which depicts

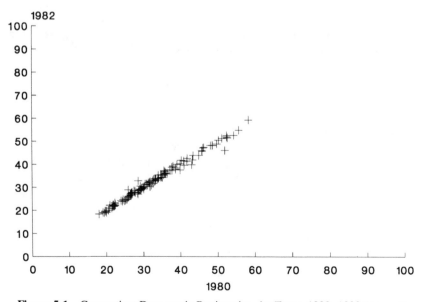

Figure 5.1   Connecticut Democratic Registration, by Town, 1980–1982 (percent)

Table 5.3 Simple Registration Equation Values

State	t	α	β	R-square
Connecticut				
	1974	2.65	0.93	0.957
	1976	2.00	0.95	0.980
	1978	0.00	0.95	0.964
	1980	0.75	0.98	0.971
	1982	0.00	0.99	0.990
	1984	0.00	0.96	0.980
	1986	0.00	1.02	0.970
Massachusetts				
	1978	0.0	0.97	0.958
	1980	3.5	0.90	0.918
	1982	0.0	0.98	0.936
	1984	4.0	0.92	0.927
	1986	0.0	0.98	0.924

Note: 1972 and 1974 data not available for Massachusetts.

Democratic registration levels in Connecticut's towns in 1980 and 1982. The prediction equation for those two years reads

$$D\%1982 = 0 + 0.99D\%1980,$$

with R-square $= 0.99$. Virtually all of the towns line up in a straight line, with a slope of 1. Similarly, statewide partisan cleavages among registrants remained virtually fixed in both states from 1972 to 1986 (see tables 5.3 and 5.4).[5]

Election data portray a much less stable electorate. Whereas registration data are virtually identical in any given pair of years, congressional, state senate, and gubernatorial election results indicate a significant amount of partisan change beneath the apparently calm surface portrayed by the registration. The prediction equations for Connecticut's congressional elections indicate that marked changes occurred not only in the statewide propensity to vote Democratic (shown by the broad fluctuations in the βs) but also in the uniformity of the state's yearly partisan swings, as shown by the wide range of the value of the R-squares (see table 5.4). Clearly, *something* causes changes to occur in the

Table 5.4 Simple Congressional Equation Values

State	t	α	β	R-square
Connecticut				
	1974	39	0.34	0.193
	1976	0	1.00	0.542
	1978	21	1.73	0.746
	1980	11	0.66	0.585
	1982	0	0.85	0.430
	1984	8	0.72	0.574
	1986	-20	1.60	0.788
Massachusetts				
	1976	0	0.65	0.491
	1978	14	0.79	0.466
	1980	15	0.63	0.624
	1982	35	0.55	0.423
	1984	45	0.22	0.064
	1986	0	1.07	0.784

Note: 1974 data not available for Massachusetts.

partisan profile of the state between elections, because the relationships between party vote in any two years is quite variable (as shown by the differences in the prediction equation values) and sometimes quite weak (as shown by the rather low R-squares). The strength of the R-square notwithstanding, what general changes seem to appear?

In 1972, a majority of Connecticut towns voted Republican. In the following election, a marked pro-Democratic surge occurred, which gradually receded until 1982, when the Democrats rallied. In 1984, the momentum shifted, producing a pro-Republican shift. Finally, in 1986, a statewide polarization resulted in a significant decrease in the number of competitive towns.

A particularly striking shift occurred between 1974 and 1976. The statewide prediction equation (see figure 5.2) was

$$D\%1976 = 0 + 1D\%1974,$$

indicating that we would expect the Democratic percentage of the congressional vote in any given town to have been the same in both years. However, the

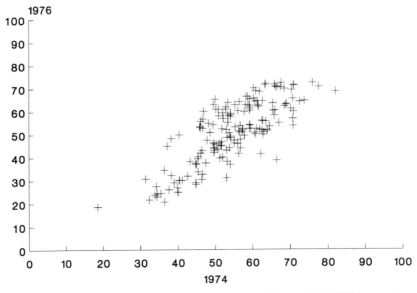

Figure 5.2 Connecticut Democratic Registration, by Town, 1974–1976 (percent)

R-square was only 0.542, indicating that there is a substantial amount of error in using this prediction equation. In other words, a significant number of towns *did not* vote in the same way, despite the prediction equation's suggestion that voting patterns were consistent.

Figure 5.3 shows that in 1974, roughly half of the towns cast between 50 percent and 60 percent of their votes for Democratic congressional candidates; in 1976, barely one-third did so. Much of the partisan shift was canceled out by equal but opposite shifts. Although the prediction equation reads

$$D\%1976 = 0 + 1D\%1974,$$

we see that it actually divides the data points, with most falling significantly above or below it. By comparison, the same prediction equation for Democratic registration percentages in 1980 and 1982 (figure 5.1) is accompanied by a much denser packing of data points. Thus, while the prediction equation indicates a politically cohesive state when applied to 1980 and 1982 registration data, the same equation with regard to congressional voting behavior in 1974 and 1976 portrays quite the opposite.

Congressional data confirm that the Massachusetts electorate also votes in a manner radically different from that suggested by the registration data. The prediction equations (table 5.4) again depict an electorate more volatile than the

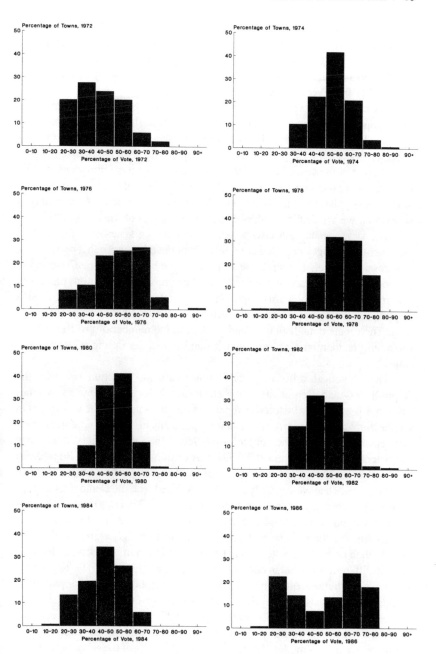

Figure 5.3 Democratic Vote, Connecticut Congressional Elections, 1972–1986

relatively stable registration levels would suggest. Although the R-squares for Massachusetts are somewhat more consistent than for Connecticut, their fluctuation, along with the large shifts in the αs and βs, shows that the propensity to vote Democratic and the statewide uniformity of that propensity do indeed vary remarkably from year to year.

Connecticut's towns are distributed unimodally, shifting back and forth in their propensity to vote Democratic; these partisan shifts vary in their statewide impact. The distribution of Massachusetts's town is startlingly bimodal, its variations occurring only in the extent to which the state is polarized (figure 5.4). In five of the seven years of this study, the towns were bimodally distributed. In the two exceptional years—1976 and 1980—the state's towns were slightly less polarized but still retained their bimodal character. Accordingly, it seems that we are dealing with not one but two states of Massachusetts.

The state senate data also portray electorates in states of constant flux; however the changes depicted are not so pronounced as those that occur at the congressional level. In fact, close analysis of the behavior of the Connecticut electorate at the state senate level indicates that presidential elections play a key role in determining the partisan profile of the state: simply put, Connecticut's Republicans come out to vote only during presidential election years (see table 5.1). The senate data display a marked shift in the number of pro-Republican towns in presidential elections, which number recedes during midterm elections.

These cyclical shifts in party fortunes call into question just who the Republicans- and Democrats-in-the-electorate really are at any given time. Table 5.1 is especially instructive regarding the shifts in Republican fortunes in Connecticut and the question of counting partisans in order to determine their fair representation. At the congressional level, the Democratic vote is fairly consistent from year to year (627,694 plus or minus 48,523); the Republican vote undergoes swings as broad as 22 percent (565,880 plus or minus 125,836). The two parties behave similarly at the state senate level, the Democrats averaging 613,129 votes a year (plus or minus 48,142, or 8.3 percent) and the Republicans swinging wildly (564,865 plus or minus 129,468, or 23 percent). In Massachusetts, the influence of presidential elections has a greater effect on turnout than on partisan vote totals. The voting pattern in state senate elections is quite different from that in congressional elections (see table 5.1). The simple statewide prediction equation values (table 5.5) display the familiar pattern of marked shifts in partisan propensity and cohesiveness from year to year. State senate data (figures 5.5 and 5.6) help to explain this. Whereas the congressional electorate varied in its polarization, towns in the state senate electorate remained constantly bimodal. The moderating influences of the surge in Republican votes in presidential election years is noticeably absent at the senatorial level (table 5.2). As a result, the distribution of towns does not shift so much at the state senate level as in congressional elections.

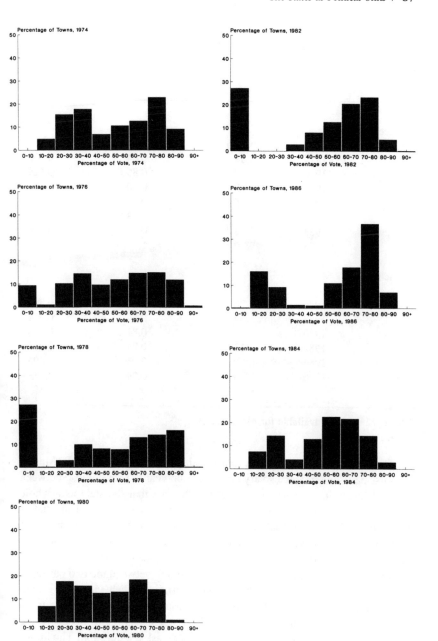

Figure 5.4   Democratic Vote, Massachusetts Congressional Elections, 1974–1986

Table 5.5 Simple State Senate Equation Values

State	t	α	β	R-square
Connecticut				
	1974	18	0.84	0.600
	1976	0	0.85	0.629
	1978	10	0.90	0.717
	1980	5.6	0.79	0.678
	1982	0	1.03	0.795
	1984	4.4	0.71	0.786
	1986	0	1.40	0.605
Massachusetts				
	1976	28	0.53	0.398
	1978	32	0.54	0.351
	1980	10	0.81	0.578
	1982	13	0.74	0.711
	1984	0	0.93	0.605
	1986	0	0.94	0.633

Note: 1972 data not available for Massachusetts.

How, then, can we describe partisanship in the two states? In Massachusetts, partisan tendencies vary not only from year to year but also between electoral levels in the same year. Despite the fact that the state as a whole remains firmly Democratic (as indicated by the party's control of the state's legislature and congressional delegation), the partisan shifts that occur within and between election years indicate that voters are *not* consistently attracted to the Democratic party label.

In Connecticut, cyclical vacillation in strength between the two parties at the senatorial level, coupled with the radical variation in behavior from year to year at the congressional level, raises the question: Which data should we use to determine the state's partisan profile? Clearly, the answer to Who are the parties-in-the-electorate? depends upon when we ask the question. The implications of this fact for partisan representation are significant. The redistricting that followed the 1980 census also immediately followed a presidential election; as a result, the preponderance of Republicans appeared high. In a nonpresidential election year, unless the Republicans experience an atypical surge

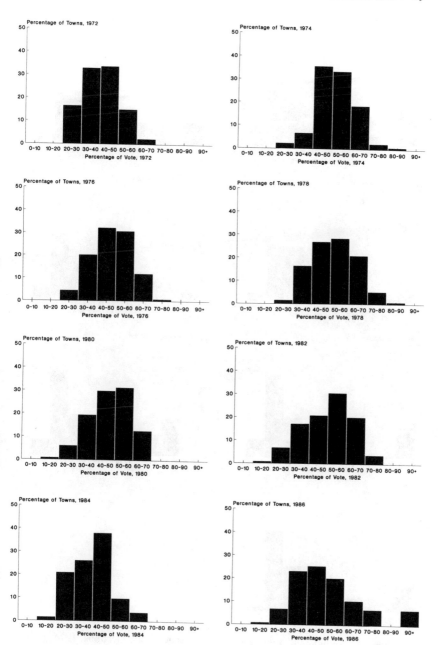

Figure 5.5 Democratic Vote, Connecticut State Senate Elections, 1972–1986

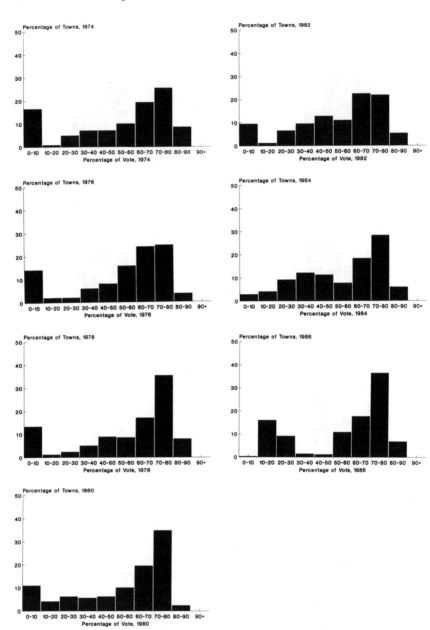

Figure 5.6 Democratic Vote, Massachusetts State Senate Elections, 1974–1986

in participation relative to the Democrats, their numbers will likely be much lower and party strength will thus appear weaker.[6]

Gubernatorial Data

For both states, there are fewer gubernatorial data to analyze, because these elections occur less frequently than either congressional or state senatorial contests. The prediction equations for Connecticut indicate that the propensity to vote Democratic varies significantly from election to election (see table 5.6). Nonetheless, the increasing values of the R-squares indicate that the state behaved in an increasingly cohesive manner throughout this period. The striking aspect of the Connecticut data is the change that seems to have occurred between 1978 and 1982. Although the prediction equation indicates that the statewide propensity to vote Democratic was virtually identical during these two years ($\beta = 0.98$), the R-square of only 0.573 indicates again that a significant number of towns changed their partisan behavior.

This is not surprising. In 1974 and 1978, Ella Grasso was the Democratic candidate for governor, while in 1982 and 1986 the candidate was William O'Neill. The gubernatorial data (figures 5.7 and 5.8) show that the Democrats' attraction of voters in 1978 was tempered in 1982, when Grasso retired and was replaced on the ticket by William O'Neill. Although the Democrats maintained control of the governorship, the change in candidates obviously resulted in

Table 5.6 Simple Statewide Gubernatorial Equation Values

State	t	α	β	R-square
Connecticut				
	1978	24	0.60	0.432
	1982	0	0.98	0.573
	1986	17	0.76	0.831
Massachusetts				
	1978	5	0.76	0.433
	1982	44	0.18	0.080
	1986	26	0.70	0.481

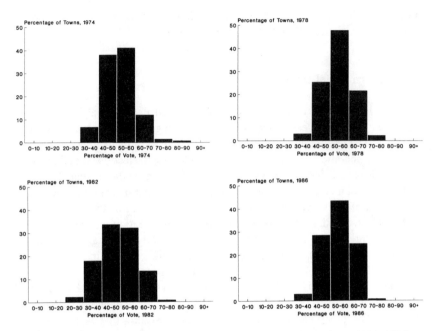

Figure 5.7 Democratic Vote, Connecticut Gubernatorial Elections, 1974–1986

shifting partisan behavior. In 1986, however, O'Neill's incumbency was met with a renewed pro-Democratic shift similar to that experienced by Grasso in 1974–78.

The conclusions to be drawn from the Massachusetts gubernatorial data are as restricted as Connecticut's because of the relatively small number of elections that occurred during the period of this study. Nonetheless, the gubernatorial equations portray an electorate by no means predictable or consistent in its partisan behavior. Despite the fact that the Democrats won all four elections between 1974 and 1986 (three of which were won by Michael Dukakis), the prediction equations do not portray any consistent statewide partisan behavior, and the R-squares indicate a fragmented electorate (see table 5.6). The pro-Republican shift that occurred when Edward King won in 1978 (see figure 5.8) was reversed in 1982, when Dukakis was reelected, to such an extent that the prediction equation accounts for a mere 8 percent of the variance in the predicted vote.[7] When Dukakis went on to win in 1986, the low R-square indicates that the increase in his support was by no means uniform statewide.

Analysis

The behavior of Massachusetts and Connecticut at the gubernatorial level is especially illuminating. The statewide propensity to support one party or the

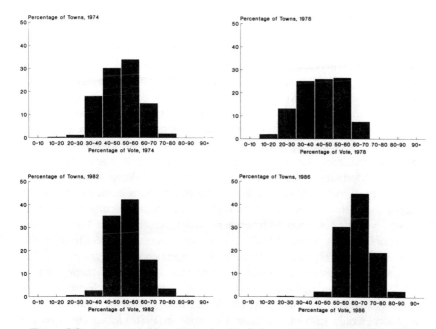

Figure 5.8   Democratic Vote, Massachusetts Gubernatorial Elections, 1974–1986

other varied markedly from one election to the next, as did the states' cohesiveness. Two conclusions can be drawn from the gubernatorial data regarding the analysis of state partisanship. First, states are not necessarily cohesive political units. States can, in fact, be quite heterogeneous. Although regression equations can be constructed to suggest that a state's partisan behavior in one election can be used to predict its behavior in the next, analysis of these equations shows that the statewide pattern of partisan change provides a poor indicator of the behavior of its subdivisions. States may therefore serve as consistent, convenient geographic references, but they are not consistent units of political analysis.

This heterogeneity of partisan behavior within a state leads to a second conclusion. Partisan behavior itself is not necessarily a consistent phenomenon. Even when the two states appeared consistent and cohesive in their patterns of partisan registration, their electoral behavior reflected opposite patterns. This suggests that factors other than past partisan behavior affect voting behavior in any given election. Although we may measure a town's partisan profile on the basis of election results, that partisan measure may be a function merely of the appeal of the candidates—not of any partisan predisposition on the part of the voters. Accordingly, a vote for a particular party's candidate may not be tantamount to an expression of support for the party. This conclusion is reinforced by the fact that, while registration levels remained virtually constant, partisan electoral results fluctuated wildly.

This is an especially important consideration. The use of partisan electoral results may be a convenient means of constructing a state's partisan profile; but this profile in fact tells us little about the true partisan behavior of the state or its subdivisions. Individual legislative and congressional districts are likely to be as insulated as individual towns from apparently statewide partisan swings. Therefore, any attempt to aggregate state legislative or congressional election data into a statewide measure of partisan fairness, such as a seats-votes ratio, is inappropriate and inadequate for the task of determining fair representational opportunity for a partisan group. Such measures ignore the divers independent political tendencies that are determined by district-specific circumstances.

The information presented in tables 5.1 and 5.2 demonstrates the inapplicability of such statewide measures. Despite the significant fluctuations in Republican turnout and vote in both states, the variations in statewide vote totals have little consistent effect upon partisan representation in the state legislature or Congress. A net shift of 7.5 percentage points toward the Democrats in Connecticut in 1976 had no effect on the congressional delegation's partisan composition; however, a shift of the same magnitude gained them a seat in 1978. Similarly anomalous behavior occurred in the last two elections in this study. A 9 percentage point shift to the Republicans gained them a seat in 1984; a prodemocratic shift of the same magnitude in 1986 had no effect on the delegation's partisan balance.

The behavior of Connecticut's voters in state senate elections provides a reflection of the congressional patterns. In some years, the percentage change in statewide vote closely approximates the percentage change in party control of seats in the state legislature (1978, 1980). In other years, however, a marked disparity exists. In 1974, a 27 percent (not percentage point) increase in the Democrats' share of the vote produced a 130 percent increase in the party's share of legislative seats. In 1982, a 12 percent increase in the Democrats' vote share had no effect on the senate's partisan balance. Then, in 1984, a 24 percent drop in vote share produces a 48 percent drop in the Democrats' share of senate seats.

A similar phenomenon occurs in Massachusetts and is best exemplified by the 1986 congressional elections. Despite the overall decrease of some 500,000 Republican votes (a 67 percent decrease from 1984), the Republican percentage of the congressional delegation did not change. This was due to the fact that almost half of the 250,385 Republican votes cast in 1986 went to incumbent Silvio Conte, while the others were scattered among the ten other congressional districts that were won by Democrats. A seats-votes measure would suggest that the Republicans might be overrepresented; a closer look, however, indicates merely that Conte is a popular incumbent.

Although states may be useful as geographic references, they are not necessarily helpful as units of measuring partisanship. Our analysis shows that the same state can have radically different partisan profiles from one year to the next, due to changes in the voting behavior of its towns, or it can appear to have the same profile, despite such changes. While both states remained heavily Democratic throughout the period of this study, our analysis indicates, for example, that Democratic Connecticut in 1976 is not necessarily comparable to Democratic Connecticut in 1974 or 1978.

If a state appears to behave more as a loose aggregation of polities than as a cohesive unit, we must ask, What causes the different polities to behave differently? Such variations are the result of district- and candidate-specific factors that make legislative and congressional districts unique political units.

The Impact of Redistricting
and Incumbency on Voting Behavior

Although a state may be useful as a geographic reference, it is not necessarily useful as a unit of political analysis. Massachusetts may be a geographically distinct entity, but that does not ensure that the state behaves as a cohesive political unit. One state may in fact comprise several distinct political subdivisions. The question remains, however, Are these substate areas well-defined political units, and if so, what is the basis for their distinct behavior? This is a key question because, for the purposes of gerrymandering analysis, we seek to identify, categorize, and distribute *partisan* blocs. A gerrymander requires identification of pockets of partisans that can be moved, in order to build a partisan bias into a given districting scheme.

As suggested in previous chapters, partisanship is related to the political environment. The political environment can be described by the specific conditions under which an election takes place. The categorization is based upon the following factors: (1) Is an incumbent running? (2) What is the incumbent's party? (3) Is the election contested? (4) Has redistricting occurred? We would expect the partisan behavior of a give town to be more consistent under stable political conditions than when the political environment is in a state of flux. *Stability* in this sense means that a voter's choices are comparable, if not identical, from one election to the next. Thus, partisan behavior is likely to be most consistent in districts where an incumbent runs and wins year after year. When political conditions are less stable—due, for example, to incumbent retirement or redistricting—we would expect partisan behavior to be more variable.

This view focuses on the candidates. Although election results are measured in partisan terms for the purposes of measuring the fairness of a districting plan, this analysis investigates the extent to which a given partisan result is in fact attributable to nonparty factors. The greater the impact of these nonparty factors, the less valid is any attempt to categorize a town as partisan based on electoral results. Thus, if we cannot determine a town's partisan profile, we cannot make the claim that a districting system is unfair to one of the parties, because we cannot say with certainty where the parties-in-the-electorate are located. Depending on the political circumstances, they may actually appear to be moving targets, because the partisan profiles of the various towns are not constant.

The Impact of Incumbency and Party Control of Districts

This chapter examines Connecticut and Massachusetts not as unitary polities but instead as aggregations of distinct and different congressional and legislative district environments. Each town is categorized according to the district-specific political circumstances of each election, using dummy variables that account for the divers political conditions.[1]

By incorporating these variables into the statewide prediction equations for each year in the manner discussed in chapter 4, the prediction error—as measured by the R-square—can be greatly reduced, in some cases as much as 300%. (See, for example, Connecticut's 1972–74 congressional prediction equation.) Use of these variables indicates that statewide measures of partisanship are illusory. They are, in fact, artifices of questionable value and meaning, since their construction overlooks the extremely significant impact of district-specific political conditions on the partisan behavior of towns.

Connecticut Congressional Elections

Several conclusions are immediately apparent from the following figures. First, the overall distribution of towns in both states varies radically from one year to the next. This is shown both by the differences in the statewide prediction equations and by the obvious differences in the scattering of towns in each figure. Second, and perhaps even more striking, is the importance that district-specific conditions play in determining partisan behavior. Looking at figure 6.1, which depicts the changes in Connecticut's Democratic congressional vote between the 1972 and 1974 elections, we see clearly that a town's propensity to increase, decrease, or maintain its Democratic share of the vote varied significantly in relation to the political environment.

Each line drawn through the points corresponds to one of the prediction equations and represents a unique set of district conditions. The statewide prediction equation (line 1), however, is quite error prone, as indicated by the R-square of 0.193.

In the complete equation that incorporates district-specific conditions, *cdem* is a dummy variable representing the partisan bias in districts controlled by the Democrats (either held by Democratic incumbents or retained by Democrats despite the retirement or the nonexistence of an incumbent), and *cincr* refers to the bias in districts in which a Republican incumbent ran. The third

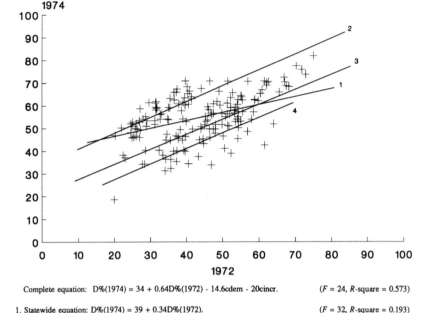

Complete equation: $D\%(1974) = 34 + 0.64D\%(1972) - 14.6cdem - 20cincr.$ ($F = 24$, R-square $= 0.573$)

1. Statewide equation: $D\%(1974) = 39 + 0.34D\%(1972)$.   ($F = 32$, R-square $= 0.193$)

2. Steele (R) retires (Republicans lose district).

3. Democrats win (includes District vacated by Grasso).

4. Republican incumbent wins.

Figure 6.1 Distribution of Democratic Vote, by Town, Connecticut Congressional Elections, 1972–1974

political environment that existed in 1974 was in a district where a Republican incumbent had retired (line 2 on figure 6.1). However, since the use of dummy variables requires only that we account for all but one of the conditions, there is no need to incorporate it into the analysis because this dummy variable's value and the corresponding prediction equation can be inferred.[2]

The three distinct political environments are represented clearly by equations 2, 3, and 4. In the Second District (line 2), where Republican incumbent Robert Steele retired, towns displayed the greatest propensity to increase their Democratic share of the vote. This suggests that Republicans had held the district due to Steele's own popularity as much as to his partisan affiliation. As soon as he retired, the Republican proportion of the vote plummeted.

In the four districts where incumbents were reelected, we see a pattern that is not surprising. Towns in Democratic districts (line 3) were five percentage points more Democratic than those in the Fifth District, held by a Republican incumbent (line 4). Although this might be expected, a closer look at the distribution of towns reveals the power of incumbency. Virtually all of the towns in the Republican Fifth District fall below the line where 1974 equals 1972, while virtually all of the points in the Democratic districts fall above it. This indicates that in districts held by incumbents, the portion of the vote for the incumbent's party tended to increase. Towns in Democratic districts tended to be slightly more Democratic in 1974 than in 1972, and towns in the Republican's district tended to be less so. Thus, we see that incumbents increase their party's percentage of the vote.

What is especially striking about Connecticut's partisan changes between 1972 and 1974 is the radically different responses that occurred in districts in which incumbents had retired. We have already noted that when Steele retired the Democratic vote jumped. As a result, we might expect to see a similar jump in the opposite direction with the retirement of a Democratic incumbent. However, this was not the case. After 1972, Democrat Ella Grasso retired from the First District to run for governor. Despite her retirement, the district behaved in the same manner as the three other districts held by Democratic incumbents. Thus, in contrast to the behavior of the towns in Steele's district, the First District's towns seemed to be more staunchly partisan: the candidate was not as important as the candidate's partisan affiliation.

By contrast, if we look at Connecticut's congressional behavior between 1976 and 1978 (figure 6.2), we see a much denser clustering of towns. As shown by the R-square of 0.746, the statewide prediction equation accounts for 75 percent of the variance in the towns' behavior—district-specific conditions notwithstanding. This suggests that all the towns had roughly the same propensity to change the Democratic proportion of their congressional vote and that the state behaved more or less as a cohesive unit.

Virtually all of the towns fall above the line where 1978 equals 1976, indicating a statewide swing toward the Democrats. Nonetheless, when we account for the conditions in the respective congressional districts, we see that the statewide equation is again misleading. However, when we account for the different district-specific conditions, we get the complete equation, where *crl* is a dummy variable representing the impact of Republican incumbent Ronald Sarasin's retirement on the Fifth District (which the Republicans subsequently lost).

In all the other districts, which were held by Democratic incumbents, the Democratic percentage of the vote increased, as described by line 3. However, the increase in Sarasin's district was even more marked, as shown by line 2. Again, we see an incumbency effect. As long as Sarasin ran, the Fifth District was Republican; as soon as he retired, the Democratic vote jumped so high that the Republicans lost the district. The increase in the R-square produced by accounting for the district conditions is considerable was well, accounting for the extraordinary shift that occurred in Sarasin's district.

These two examples show that statewide measures of partisanship can be

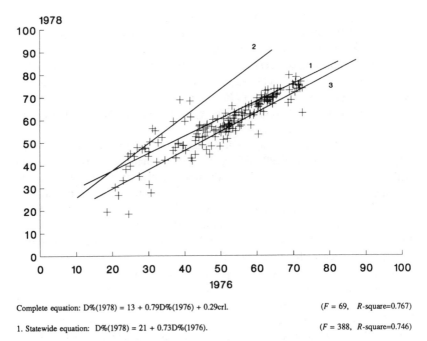

Complete equation: D%(1978) = 13 + 0.79D%(1976) + 0.29crl.　　　　　　(F = 69,　R-square=0.767)

1. Statewide equation:　D%(1978) = 21 + 0.73D%(1976).　　　　　　(F = 388,　R-square=0.746)

2. Sarasin (R) retires (Republicans lose district).

3. all other districts.

Figure 6.2　Distribution of Democratic Vote, by Town, Connecticut Congressional Elections, 1976–1978

misleading. A state's component parts can vary markedly in their behavior from one year to the next. Furthermore, the relationship among them is by no means constant. In some years (1974, for example), the state behaves as a loose aggregation; in others (1978, for example), it appears as a much more cohesive political unit.

Connecticut State Senate Elections

These general patterns are present at the state senate level as well. From one year to the next, we see varying incumbency effects on the partisan vote, as well as shifts in the state's cohesion. Figures 6.3 and 6.4, which chart Connecticut's electoral behavior in the 1972–74 and 1976–78 state senate elections, respectively, reinforce our conclusions about the impact of district and candidate factors on partisan voting behavior. In both years, the state acted in a fairly cohesive manner (as shown by high R-squares). Although the addition of dis-

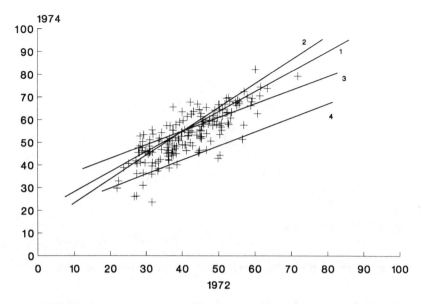

Complete equation: D%(1974) = 30 + 0.57D%(1972) +0.42sdiw -17.4sincd -12.7sincr   (*F* =41, *R*-square=0.696)

1. Statewide equation: D%(1974) = 18 + 0.84D%(1972).   (*F* = 198, *R*-square=0.600)

2. Democrat incumbents win.

3. Republicans lose retired incumbents' districts.

4. Republican incumbents win.

Figure 6.3   Distribution of Democratic Vote, by Town, Connecticut State Senate Elections, 1972–1974

trict and candidate factors caused some improvement in the explanatory capacity of the simple equations, their effect is hardly as pronounced as it was in the 1972–74 congressional results (figure 6.1).

Although the 1974 statewide equation accounts for 60 percent of the variance (*R*-square = 0.600), accounting for district conditions increases the accuracy of our predictions by almost 16 percent, to *R*-square = 0.696. In this case, the dummy variables are of two types. *Sdiw* is a coefficient dummy that refers to districts where Democratic incumbents won; *sincd* and *sincr* are intercept variables, representing the bias that may result from the presence of Democratic and Republican incumbents, respectively. In figure 6.4, *sdw* and *sdem* are coefficient and intercept variables that refer to districts held by the Democrats. In both cases, we see an incumbent effect (figure 6.3, line 3, and figure 6.4, line 4). We also see indications that the senatorial districts behave independently of any apparent stateside partisan shifts, although this independence is less pronounced than that displayed by the congressional districts.

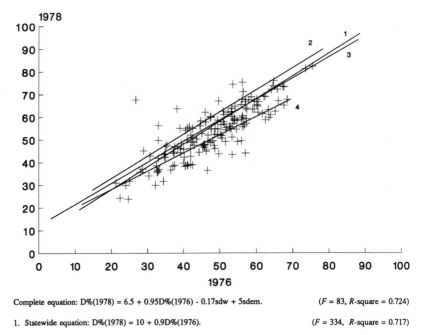

Complete equation: D%(1978) = 6.5 + 0.95D%(1976) - 0.17sdw + 5sdem.   (F = 83, R-square = 0.724)

1. Statewide equation: D%(1978) = 10 + 0.9D%(1976).   (F = 334, R-square = 0.717)

2. Democrat incumbents win.

3. Republican incumbents run (win or lose).

4. Democrats hold retired incumbent's district.

Figure 6.4   Distribution of Democratic Vote, by Town, Connecticut State Senate Elections, 1976–1978

The variable impact of different political environments suggests that partisan propensity can vary significantly from constituency to constituency, district to district, and year to year. A state that employs a district system of representation thus can have as many unique constituencies as legislative districts. What happens, however, when political conditions change as a result of redistricting?

The Impact of Redistricting in Connecticut

Whereas only six towns were redistricted at the congressional level, eighteen were redistricted at the state senate level. This larger number permits us to examine the effects of redistricting on partisan behavior in Connecticut. The changes in partisan behavior that occurred in redistricted towns suggest that partisan behavior in a previous election can be an almost meaningless factor in determining ensuing electoral behavior. This finding challenges prevailing assumptions about representation, partisanship, and gerrymandering. Many analysts assume that one way to gerrymander a particular group is to divide its voters and distribute them in a manner that prevents them from forming a majority-sized bloc. It is also assumed that we can get rid of a particular legislator simply by moving a sufficient number of voters into the district who do not support that legislator's party.

These scenarios presuppose that the voters in the redistricted constituencies will maintain their partisan profile. That is, they will be just as Democratic or Republican in their new district as they were in their old one. The data show, however, that this is simply not the case. In face, all redistricted towns display one common characteristic: regardless of their previous partisan behavior, they all experienced increases in partisan vote levels for the party or incumbent controlling their new district.

Figure 6.5, which presents the changes in the Democratic proportion of the state senate vote from 1980 to 1982, illustrates the effects of redistricting. Towns that were moved from Republican to Democratic districts (line 3) showed an increase in the Democratic percentage of their vote that was actually higher than that displayed by the towns that remained in districts held by Democratic incumbents (line 4).

Not surprisingly, the largest increases in the Democratic proportion of the vote occurred in the district where a Republican incumbent retired (line 2). Relatively speaking, the retirement of the incumbent had a greater effect than the removal of an incumbent by redistricting. Nonetheless, redistricting had a marked effect on the partisan vote. This is especially evident in the behavior of towns moved from Democratic to Republican districts (line 6), where the Democratic proportion of the vote in the affected towns tended to drop 16 percent.

The impact of district-specific conditions on partisan behavior and the changes associated with the 1980–82 redistricting in Connecticut are by no means earthshaking. Nonetheless they are significant: towns behave differently when their political environments change. Whether these changes are due to incumbent retirement or redistricting is less important for our purposes than the fact that redistricted towns respond to the changes in a nonrandom manner. Such partisan change indicates that, contrary to the logic of and assertions made in Court cases and by some political scientists, we cannot assume that the electoral environment is an insignificant determinant of partisan behavior.

Specifically, neither the political parties nor the redistricted towns in Connecticut could claim to have been gerrymandered, because the towns altered their behavior in response to changes in their district and incumbent circumstances. Furthermore, the observed changes in the redistricted towns are especially striking when contrasted with turnout trends. As table 5.1 indicates, the raw statewide Republican vote for the state senate dropped 30 percent (197,382 votes) between 1980 and 1982. Yet, towns moved into Republican districts as a

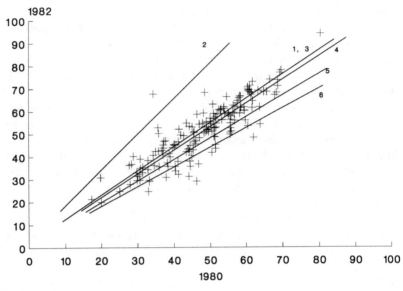

Complete equation:

$$D\%(1982) = 0 + 1.38D\%(1980) - 0.38sdiw - 0.48sriw - 0.38sdw - 0.49sdl - 0.35srw - 0.54sdr - 0.36srd$$
$$(F = 75, \ R\text{-square} = 0.844)$$

1. Statewide equation: $D\%(1982) = 0 + 1.03D\%(1980)$. $(F = 513, \ R\text{-square} = 0.795)$

2. Republicans lose retired incumbents' district.

3. Republicans hold retired incumbents' district;
   towns moved from Republican to Democrat district.

4. Democrats hold retired incumbents' district.

5. Republican incumbents win;
   Democrats lose retired incumbents' district.

6. Towns moved from Democrat to Republican district.

Figure 6.5 Distribution of Democratic Vote, by Town, Connecticut State Senate Elections, 1980–1982

result of redistricting experienced a relative *increase* in the Republican percentage of the vote. Thus, in some cases, district conditions can actually counteract apparently statewide trends.

Naturally, such behavior might be characteristic only of Connecticut. Let us examine Massachusetts (which has more than twice the number of towns) in order to verify the implications drawn from Connecticut's behavior.

Massachusetts Congressional Elections

Accounting for incumbency and party control causes as marked an improvement of the prediction equations in Massachusetts as in Connecticut.[3] The incumbency effect again appears and varies in its impact from year to year. In 1974–76 (figure 6.6), the state divided into two categories: towns in districts held by Democrats (line 2) and towns in districts held by Republicans (line 3). The retirement of Democratic incumbent Paul Tsongas (who ran for the U.S. Senate) had no noticeable effect on the behavior of the towns in his district. Line 2 portrays the behavior of towns in his district as well as those in districts held by Democratic incumbents. In the same way that Ella Grasso's retirement had no partisan effect on her constituents in Connecticut in 1974 (figure 6.1), Tsongas's retirement was similarly uneventful in Massachusetts. Thus, in 1976, who the incumbents were seemed to be less a factor than their party

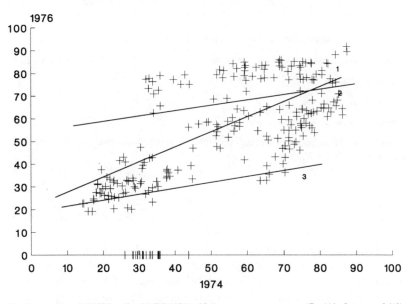

Complete equation: D%(1976) = 18 + 0.24D%(1974) + 35cdem. $(F = 116, \ R\text{-square} = 0.610)$

1. statewide equation: D%(1976) = 20 + 0.65D%(1974). $(F = 291, \ R\text{-square} = 0.491)$

2. Democrats hold district.

3. Republicans hold district.

Figure 6.6   Distribution of Democratic Vote, by Town, Massachusetts Congressional Elections, 1974–1976

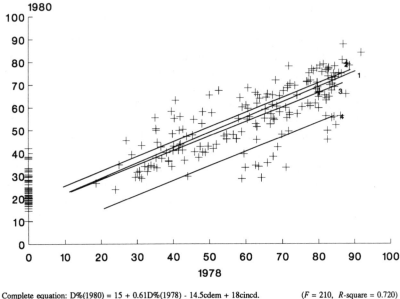

Complete equation: D%(1980) = 15 + 0.61D%(1978) - 14.5cdem + 18cincd.   (*F* = 210, *R*-square = 0.720)

1. Statewide equation: D%(1980) = 15 + 0.63D%(1978).   (*F* = 410, *R*-square = 0.624)

2. Democrat incumbents win.

3. Republican incumbents win.

4. Drinan (D) retires (Democrats hold district).

Figure 6.7   Distribution of Democratic Vote, by Town, Massachusetts Congressional Elections, 1978–1980

affiliation. We do, however, see a strong incumbent effect in 1980 (figure 6.7), 1984 (figure 6.8), and 1986 (figure 6.9).

The position of most towns below the line where 1980 equals 1978 in figure 6.7 indicates a general pro-Republican shift in 1980. However, the surge was weakest in the districts held by Democratic incumbents (line 2) and strongest in the Fourth District, where Robert Drinan retired (line 4) and was replaced by fellow Democrat Barney Frank. Although Frank held the district, the propensity to vote Democratic was even lower than that exhibited by the towns in the district held by Republican incumbent Margaret Heckler. Similarly, in 1982–84 (figure 6.8, line 3) and 1984–86 (figure 6.9, line 3), the retirement of an incumbent produced a marked change in the propensity to vote Democratic. The retirement of Democratic incumbent James Shannon was accompanied by a fourteen percentage point drop in the Democratic tally in the towns in his

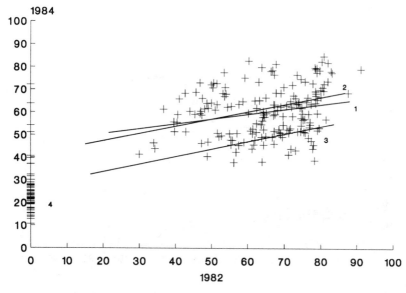

Complete equation: D%(1984) = 27 + 0.31D%(1982) + 14cincd.   ($F = 31$, R-square = 0.210)

1. Statewide equation: D%(1984) = 45 + 0.22D%(1982).   ($F = 16$, R-square = 0.064)

2. Democrat incumbents win.

3. Shannon (D) retires (Democrats hold district).

4. towns in only Republican district.

Figure 6.8   Distribution of Democratic Vote, by Town, Massachusetts Congressional Elections, 1982–1984

district (figure 6.8, line 3) relative to the towns in districts where incumbents stood for reelection (figure 6.8, line 2).

These partisan patterns are particularly striking.[4] Although one of these districts experienced the retirement of an incumbent (Shannon), all the towns nonetheless remained under Democratic control. Despite this constancy of partisan conditions statewide, the prediction equation accounts for a mere 21 percent of the variance in predicting the towns' Democratic percentage of the vote in 1984 (R-square = 0.210). Thus, even when the same party retained control of all these towns, something other than previous partisan behavior and incumbency or district factors accounted for some 79 percent of the changes in the Democratic proportion of the vote. Although electoral results may be measured in partisan terms, they are clearly not always determined by partisan considerations. Nonetheless, in 1986, previous partisan behavior, along with

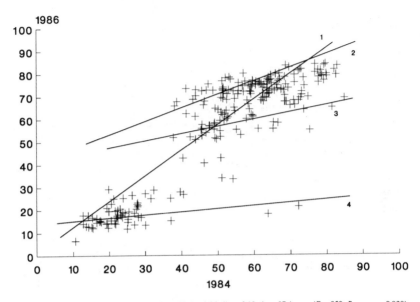

Complete equation: D%(1986) = 40 + 0.31D%(1984) + 0.26cdiw - 0.18criw - 27cinc.r   (*F* = 850, *R*-square = 0.928)

1. Statewide equation: D%(1986) = 0 + 1.07D%(1984).   (*F* = 1210, *R*-square = 0.784)

2. Democrat incumbents win.

3. O'Neill (D) retires (Democrats hold district).

4. Republican incumbent wins.

Figure 6.9   Distribution of Democratic Vote, by Town, Massachusetts Congressional Elections, 1984–1986

district and incumbency factors, accounted for 92.8 percent of the variance in predicting partisan vote, while in 1984 these factors accounted for only 21 percent of the variance. Accordingly, we cannot be certain that similar partisan electoral results from one year to the next indicate similar partisan predispositions of voters

In 1984–86 (figure 6.9), we see not only the division of the state between districts held by Democrats and Republicans but also the further division of the Democrats between districts in which incumbents ran (line 2) and in which incumbents retired (line 3). The striking aspect of this division of Democratic districts is that line 3 in figure 6.9 portrays the behavior of the towns in the district vacated by Tip O'Neill and inherited by Joseph Kennedy III. Despite the fact that the Democrats ran a new candidate with a well-known name, the district still showed a decreased propensity to vote Democratic in the wake of their incumbent's retirement.

Massachusetts State Senate Elections

The results are the same for voting behavior at the state senate level. Once again, the addition of district and incumbency variables results in a marked improvement in the strength of the prediction equations. The incumbency effect is especially impressive. Whereas we observe the usual decrease in the propensity to support the retired incumbents' party in 1980 (figure 6.10, line 5) and 1986 (figure 6.12, line 3), we see radical shifts in partisan propensities in 1982 in the Second Hampden and Hampshire (figure 6.11, line 5) and the Second Worcester and Middlesex (figure 6.12, line 2) Districts.

The Second Hampden and Hampshire District (see table 6.1) was a Democratic stronghold throughout the period studied (that is, Democrats won all

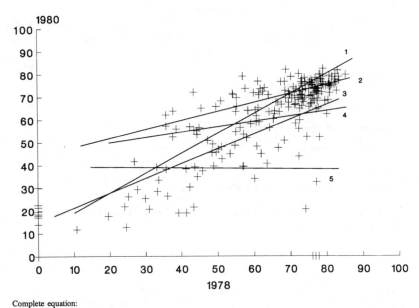

Complete equation:
D%(1980) = 14 + 0.64D%(1978) - 0.27sdiw - 0.39sdw - 0.66sdl + 30sdem.   (*F* = 123, *R*-square = 0.727)

1. Statewide equation: D%(1980) = 10 + 0.81D%(1978).   (*F* = 388, *R*-square = 0.578)

2. Democrat incumbent wins.

3. Republicans hold retired incumbent's district.

4. Democrats hold retired incumbent's district.

5. Democrats lose retired incumbent's district.

Figure 6.10 Distribution of Democratic Vote, by Town, Massachusetts State Senate Elections, 1978–1980

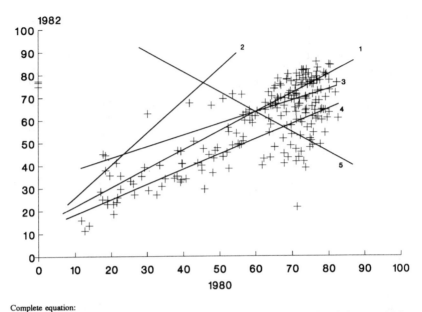

Complete equation:
D%(1982) = 1 - 0.85D%(1980) + 1.33sdiw + 1.48sriw + 2.15srw + 106sdem - 84sincd.   (F = 143, R-square = 0.747)

1. Statewide equation: D%(1982) = 13 + 0.74D%(1980)   (F = 466, R-square = 0.711)

2. Republicans hold retired incumbent's district (2nd Worcester & Middlesex).

3. Democrat incumbent wins.

4. Republican incumbent wins.

5. Democrats hold retired incumbent's district (2nd Hampden & Hampshire).

Figure 6.11   Distribution of Democratic Vote, by Town, Massachusetts State Senate Elections, 1980–1982

contests). The data cast doubt, however, on the extent to which the district and its constituent towns can actually be labeled Democratic. If we look only at vote totals, the district's partisan profile appears to be quite volatile, despite the fact that it remained in Democratic hands. It was overwhelmingly partisan in 1980 and 1984 and quite competitive in 1982. This partisan fluctuation was due to changes in the cast of characters on election day.

Alan Sisitsky, a strong incumbent who had held his seat for several elections, won an uncontested election in 1980 before retiring. Voters, however, might not have been as pleased with Sisitsky as the vote totals indicate. Looking at tables 6.1 and 6.2 and figure 6.12, we see that when Sisitsky was unchallenged, his victories were also characterized by variable turnouts. When Sisitsky had last been challenged in 1974 (in the erstwhile Hampden and Berkshire District), he defeated his opponent handily (29,805 to 11,154). Unchallenged in that district in 1976, he tallied some 43,000 votes.

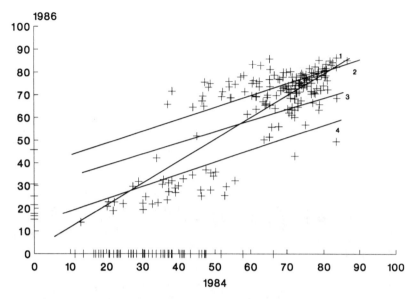

Complete equation: D%(1986) = 12.5 + 0.50D%(1984) + 14sdem + 12sincd.   ($F = 362$, R-square = 0.813)

1. Statewide equation: D%(1986) = 0 + 0.94D%(1984).   ($F = 434$, R-square = 0.633)

2. Democrat incumbent wins.

3. Democrats hold retired incumbent's district.

4. Republican incumbents win.

Figure 6.12   Distribution of Democratic Vote, by Town, Massachusetts State Senate Elections, 1984–1986

In the new Second Hampden and Hampshire District (created in the 1976 redistricting), Sisitsky continued to receive an overwhelming percentage of the vote in 1978 and 1980, due in part to the fact that he was unchallenged. As table 6.2 indicates, however, voters who had abstained from voting when Sisitsky was unchallenged were mobilized after his retirement in 1982 by the opportunity to vote for the first Republican challenger in eight years. Whereas the number of abstentions hovered between 10,000 and 15,000 when Sisitsky (and later, his successor, Linda Melconian) ran unopposed, the contested election in 1982 lowered this number to a mere 2,824 (see table 6.2). Thus, when the district appeared to be most heavily Democratic, some 30 percent of the electorate did not bother to cast a ballot. In the one competitive contest that occurred during this period (1982), only 6.62 percent of the voters abstained, and the Republicans garnered 38 percent of the vote.

Table 6.1 State Senate Votes by Town, Massachusetts Second Hampden and Hampshire District, 1980-1984 Elections

Town	1980 Election		1982 Election		1984 Election	
	Democrat	Republican	Democrat	Republican	Democrat	Republican
Agawam	7,718	0	4,943	2,895	8,214	0
Blandford	373	0	166	218	366	0
Chester	389	0	217	126	369	0
Chesterfield	279	0	141	137	326	0
Cummington	289	0	141	144	272	0
Goshen	227	0	124	106	266	0
Granville	444	0	219	271	399	0
Huntington	601	0	275	256	451	0
Longmeadow	6,551	0	2,727	3,972	6,050	0
Middlefield	134	0	68	56	132	0
Montgomery	277	0	143	110	255	0
Plainfield	142	0	75	72	157	0
Russell	484	0	249	182	447	0
Southwick	2,344	0	1,466	761	2,498	0
Tolland	106	0	43	51	97	0
W. Springfield	8,976	0	5,351	3,703	8,531	0
Westhampton	407	0	223	205	470	0
Worthington	356	0	168	195	341	0

Table 6.2 State Senate Vote Totals, Massachusetts Second Hampden and Hampshire District, 1978-1986 Elections

| Year | Democrat | Republican | Other | Blank | Total | | Percentages | |
						Democrat	Republican	Blank
1978	28,548	0	14	11,010	39,572	72.14	0	27.82
1980	38,666	0	6	15,936	54,608	70.81	0	29.18
1982	23,533	16,281	11	2,824	42,649	55.18	38.17	6.62
1984	38,416	0	6	16,937	54,359	70.67	0	31.15
1986	25,315	0	5	8,460	33,778	74.95	0	25.05

Note: I was unable to acquire ward and precinct data from West Springfield, parts of which are included in the Second Hampden and Hampshire District. Consequently, the vote totals of table 6.1 do not agree with the totals of table 6.2.

Table 6.3 State Senate Vote, by Town, Massachusetts Second Worcester and Middlesex District, 1978-1986 Elections

Town	1978 Election		1980 Election		1982 Election		1984 Election		1986 Election	
	Democrat	Republican	Democrat	Republican	Democrat	Republican	Democrat	Republican	Democrat	Republican
Ashburnham	0	1,050	399	1,376	622	856	527	1,346	404	917
Ashby	0	667	192	862	269	646	230	854	169	543
Bolton	0	756	304	869	337	719	339	1,094	248	767
Fitchburg	0	9,482	2,752	11,726	5,953	6,704	5,056	9,103	4,281	5,448
Gardner	0	4,566	2,404	5,213	4,496	2,445	2,731	4,612	1,776	3,061
Holden	0	4,423	1,369	5,018	2,347	3,314	1,851	5,074	1,241	3,912
Lancaster	0	1,347	555	1,634	708	1,168	542	1,826	301	1,219
Leominster	0	8,417	2,638	10,536	5,435	6,291	4,042	8,767	3,016	5,823
Lunenburg	0	2,414	582	3,468	501	3,140	545	3,615	402	2,422
Princeton	0	725	251	907	382	648	283	1,044	234	817
Sterling	0	1,479	608	1,839	882	1,272	645	2,078	390	1,441
Townsend	0	1,475	666	2,008	980	1,436	755	2,477	426	1,463
Westminster	0	1,578	559	2,007	887	1,312	695	1,967	497	1,345

Table 6.4 State Senate Vote Totals, Massachusetts Second Worcester and Middlesex District, 1978-1986 Elections

Year	Democrat	Republican	Other	Blank	Total	Percentages Democrat	Percentages Republican	Percentages Blank
1978	0	38,379	31	11,546	49,956	0	76.8	23.11
1980	13,279	47,463	6	4,883	65,631	20.23	72.3	7.44
1982	23,799	29,951	13	2,382	56,145	42.38	53.3	4.24
1984	18,241	43,857	4	3,540	65,642	27.78	66.8	5.39
1986	13,385	29,178	0	2,797	45,360	29.51	64.3	6.16

A cursory study of vote totals indicates that Sisitsky had been immensely popular. An examination of the abstention rate, however, suggests that a significant number of bored or perhaps disaffected voters chose to abstain rather than vote for an unchallenged incumbent. A similar phenomenon occurred in the Second Worcester and Middlesex District, which was held by Republicans. The retirement of Republican incumbent Robert Hall resulted in a closely contested race in 1982 (see tables 6.3 and 6.4). When Hall, who had been unopposed in 1978, was challenged in 1980, abstaining voters were mobilized and voted for his opponent, but there were few defections from Hall's camp, and he won by a wide margin. Hall's retirement in 1982, however, resulted in massive defections. His Republican successor, Mary Padua, withstood the 1982 Democratic challenge and reestablished a firm (albeit somewhat smaller) Republican majority in the district, easily defeating successive challengers in 1984 and 1986.

The data from these two state senatorial districts indicate again that the political conditions on election day play a large part in determining a constituency's partisan profile. The overwhelming partisan margins in these two districts were due in no small part to the fact that the incumbents were unchallenged. When conditions changed and the incumbents either retired or were challenged, the districts' partisanship became significantly less one-sided. In both cases, the retired incumbent's party retained its control over the district; yet the partisan profile of the voting constituencies underwent significant transformation.

Both districts remained loyal to one party (or, more accurately, they voted for candidates bearing the same party label). Nonetheless, the shifting partisan profile of both districts indicates that the extent to which these districts could be labeled partisan is a matter of debate. This variability is significant because when and under what conditions the partisan profile of a given constituency is measured determine how it is labeled and, therefore, whether one of the parties has been gerrymandered.

The Impact of Redistricting in Massachusetts

In Massachusetts, redistricting of the two sets of legislative districts occurs in different years. The congressional redistricting occurs early in each decade, shortly after the decennial census. The state legislative districts, however, are redrawn in middecade. Accordingly, new district lines affected the 1976 state senate election and the 1982 congressional election.

Massachusetts, with a greater number of towns and districts, provides a larger sample of constituencies affected by redistricting than Connecticut; sixty-nine towns were moved among congressional districts, and sixty towns were moved across state senate lines. At both levels, as in Connecticut, the redistricted towns experienced marked shifts toward the party controlling their new district.

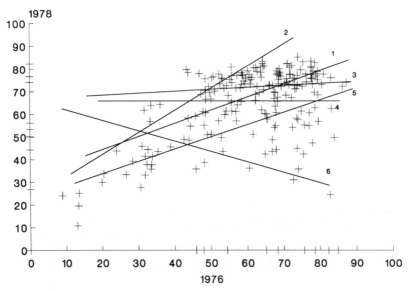

Complete equation:
D%(1978) = 22 + 0.91D%(1976) - 0.81sdiw - 0.38srw - 0.87sdw - 1.33sdr + 43sdem.   (F = 83, R-square = 0.685)

1. Statewide equation: D%(1978) = 32 + 0.54D%(1976).   (F =148, R-square = 0.351)

2. Towns moved from Republican to Democrat districts; Republicans lose retired incumbent's district.

3. Democrat incumbent wins.

4. Democrats hold retired incumbent's district.

5. Republican incumbents win.

6. Towns moved from Democrat to Republican districts.

Figure 6.13   Distribution of Democratic Vote, by Town, Massachusetts Congressional Elections, 1976–1978

In the state senate (figure 6.13), towns that were moved from Democratic to Republican districts (line 6) became significantly more Republican, and those moved from Republican to Democratic districts (line 2) moved toward the Democrats as markedly as those in districts where the Republicans lost a retired incumbent's district. In the congressional elections of 1982 (figure 6.14), the effects of redistricting were dramatic. Although there was a statewide surge toward the Democrats from 1980 to 1982 (shown by the preponderance of towns above the X = Y line), the strength of the shift was tempered by the political conditions in the various districts.

Towns that were moved from Republican to Democratic districts (line 4) displayed a propensity to vote Democratic almost as high as that of towns that had remained in districts held by Democratic incumbents (line 3). Since there were no open seats, this shift is especially noteworthy because these redistricted

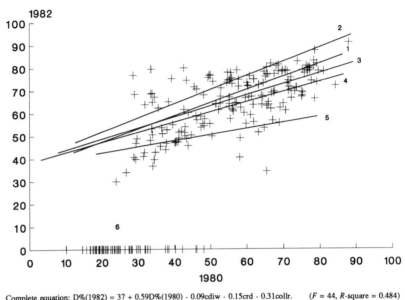

Complete equation: D%(1982) = 37 + 0.59D%(1980) - 0.09cdiw - 0.15crd - 0.31collr. ($F = 44$, R-square = 0.484)

1. Statewide equation: D%(1982) = 35 + 0.55D%(1980) ($F = 176$, R-square = 0.423)

2. Towns moved between Democrat districts; towns moved from Democrat to collapsed district.

3. Democrat incumbent wins.

4. Towns moved from Republican to Democrat districts.

5. Towns moved from Republican to collapsed district.

6. Towns in only Republican district

Figure 6.14 Distribution of Democratic Vote, by Town, Massachusetts Congressional Elections, 1980–1982

towns, which had been in Heckler's district, behaved in 1982 almost as if they had always been in a Democrat's district.

Towns that were moved from Democratic districts to the one remaining Republican district (Silvio Conte's) experienced a marked drop in Democratic votes because Conte ran unopposed. However, it should be noted that these towns, once moved, started to vote for Conte as strongly as the towns that had always been in his district (see table 6.5). The partisan transformation represents an almost total reversal of previous voting patterns in the redistricted towns. Towns that voted 2:1 Democratic in 1978 and 1980, when they were in Democrat Edward Boland's district, voted 2:1 Republican in 1984 and 3:1 in 1986, in Conte's district.

Skeptics might argue that these towns had been ripe for realignment anyway and that the redistricting provided the opportunity for them to alter their partisan behavior. However, an examination of their state senate election tallies belies this contention. Table 6.6 shows that, despite the partisan conversion of these towns at the congressional level, they remained steadfastly Democratic in their state senate voting patterns. Throughout this period, their state senate district was held by the same Democratic incumbent (Robert Witmore). Accordingly, these towns experienced a massive partisan transformation at one electoral level and no change at another.

Congressional redistricting also provided the uncommon phenomenon of a collapsed district in which two incumbents (Heckler and Frank) were forced to run against each other, because the state had lost a seat in the 1980 reapportionment. In the collapsed district, a general shift toward the Democrats occurred as a result of the redistricting. Not only did the towns in Frank's original district display a remarkable increase in the propensity to vote Democratic (figure 6.14, line 2), but the towns from Heckler's old district exhibited a marked increase in their propensity to vote Democratic as well (see table 6.5 and figure 6.14, line 5).

The transformation of towns in the collapsed district is no less remarkable than that displayed by the towns absorbed by Conte's district. Heckler's towns (which had supported her by margins of 5:3 in 1978 and 3:2 in 1980), supported Frank by a narrow margin in 1982 and then became overwhelmingly Democratic in 1984 and 1986. Accordingly, predictions of Frank's demise during the 1980 redistricting process were misinformed.[5] It was commonly known that the 1982 congressional district map had been drawn, with his demise in mind, by Frank's enemies in the state legislature. In fact, Frank himself commented, "If you asked legislators to draw a map in which Barney Frank would never be a member of Congress again, this is it."[6] The new district, drawn principally from Heckler's old one, had been overwhelmingly and consistently Republican in the several elections prior to the redistricting.

However, the fact that towns in Heckler's district appeared to be Republican had as much to do with the absence of quality Democratic challengers as it did with the fact that Heckler ran as a Republican. Although Heckler still won in 1982 in many of the towns that were in her old district, the Democratic surge throughout the collapsed district shrunk her margin of victory in these towns enough that Frank was able to win the district with overwhelming victories in the few towns remaining from his old constituency.

Naturally, the persona and number of the candidates in the old and new districts have a marked effect on the changes that occur in a given town's behavior. Although the prediction equations for towns moved from Boland's district to Conte's are meaningless (since the latter was unopposed in 1982), table 6.5 shows just how quick the reversal of partisan voting patterns was in these towns. In conclusion, we can see that redistricting alone can result in marked changes in the partisan behavior of towns that are moved—especially when moved between districts controlled by different parties.

Table 6.5 Congressional Votes in Massachusetts Towns Before and After Redistricting, 1978-1986 Elections

Town	1978 Election		1980 Election		1982 Election		1984 Election		1986 Election	
	Democrat	Republican	Democrat	Republican	Democrat	Republican	Democrat	Republican	Democrat	Republican
Towns redistricted from Boland's to Conte's district										
Athol	2,323	1,131	2,067	1,193	0	3,084	1,018	3,035	535	2,233
Orange	1,055	704	1,285	793	0	1,859	619	1,985	352	1,542
Petersham	232	206	238	195	0	406	175	406	77	350
Phillipston	181	106	193	105	0	284	131	315	77	234
Royalston	178	105	166	116	0	278	137	264	71	219
Templeton	1,207	489	1,253	545	0	1,746	849	1,526	520	1,070
Winchendon	1,298	422	1,123	454	0	1,570	1,057	1,371	450	913

Towns Collapsed from Heckler's to Frank's district

Attleboro	2,652	5,887	4,024	7,993	4,268	5,848	8,492	3,869	7,029	1,095
Berkley	262	460	367	711	452	473	729	403	662	122
Fall River	12,863	16,931	15,015	18,266	18,770	11,778	27,062	4,264	19,235	1,762
Foxboro	1,757	2,787	2,665	3,772	2,616	2,881	4,036	2,416	3,455	620
Freetown	619	1,216	1,025	1,938	1,404	1,198	2,097	893	1,737	290
Mansfield	1,564	2,123	2,429	3,041	2,354	2,425	3,784	1,960	3,073	446
Medfield	1,258	2,712	1,584	3,616	2,173	2,412	3,295	2,081	3,125	415
Natick	4,380	6,635	5,575	9,085	6,982	5,708	10,648	4,408	8,284	1,259
N. Attleboro	1,881	3,705	2,910	5,049	2,479	3,871	5,435	3,040	4,258	807
Norton	1,156	1,920	1,748	2,784	1,713	2,116	2,832	1,560	2,352	454
Plainville	1,089	1,902	756	1,681	858	1,226	1,625	1,030	1,334	271
Rehoboth	801	1,384	939	2,272	1,065	1,642	2,023	1,240	1,714	370
Seekonk	1,158	2,262	1,775	3,812	2,051	2,367	3,879	1,552	2,987	428
Sharon	2,294	3,179	2,951	4,430	4,768	1,725	6,305	1,435	4,949	360
Somerset	3,292	4,203	3,991	5,241	4,473	3,657	7,395	1,774	5,582	532
Swansea	1,908	3,142	2,555	3,935	2,938	3,002	5,133	1,519	3,717	488
Wellesley	4,560	7,559	4,231	9,651	5,583	6,903	8,276	5,804	7,405	1,357
Westport	1,515	2,969	2,263	3,864	2,792	2,547	4,587	1,681	3,919	589
Wrentham	752	1,322	1,014	1,900	1,114	1,534	1,911	1,263	1,710	325

Note: Redistricting occurred after the 1980 census; therefore the 1982 election was the first congressional election affected.

Table 6.6 State Senate Votes in Conte's District Before and After Redistricting, 1978-1986 Elections

Town	1978 Election		1980 Election		1982 Election		1984 Election		1986 Election	
	Democrat	Republican	Democrat	Republican	Democrat	Republican	Democrat	Republican	Democrat	Republican
Athol	2,474	0	3,040	0	2,165	1,279	2,728	1,311	2,325	0
Orange	1,508	0	2,024	0	1,162	911	1,618	955	1,625	0
Petersham	374	0	428	0	303	180	412	163	351	0
Phillipston	249	0	345	0	211	128	273	174	260	0
Royalston	248	0	316	0	223	116	274	128	236	0
Templeton	1,560	0	2,072	0	1,556	2,193	1,622	805	1,372	0
Winchendon	1,525	0	1,967	0	1,396	493	1,688	758	1,207	0

Note: Congressional redistricting occurred after the 1980 census.

Interlevel Influence on Voting Patterns

Do electoral conditions at one level of the electorate have effects on voting patterns at other levels? On the one hand, we might expect voters in a popular congressional incumbent's district to feel a pull toward that incumbent's party when voting for governor or state senator, especially if the candidates at the other levels are not well known. On the other hand, the literature that maintains that presidential coattails have shortened and that congressional elections seem to be insulated from national political trends suggests otherwise.

In fact, the evidence of any such interlevel coattail effect is inconclusive. Most often, political conditions at one electoral level actually do serve to improve upon the predictive capacity of the simple prediction equations. However, employing the level-specific variables normally provides the most accurate prediction equations. The interlevel variables clearly have some impact on the simple prediction equations (see appendix). In fact, in two exceptional cases, they actually serve as better predictors than the level-specific variables. In 1978–80, conditions at the congressional level in Connecticut actually were better predictors of state senate voting behavior than the conditions at the state senate level. Also, in 1982–84, Massachusetts state senate conditions seemed to be better determinants of congressional voting patterns. These are the excep-

Table 6.7 Connecticut: Democratic Incumbents Reelected, Equation Values

Election	t	α	β
Congress			
1974	19.4	0.64	
1976	15.0	0.62	
1978	13.0	0.79	
1980	4.0	0.80	
1982	0.0	1.15	
1984	15.0	0.67	
1986	-9.4	1.25	
State Senate			
1974	12.6	0.99	
1976	0.0	0.83	
1978	11.5	0.95	
1980	7.0	0.78	
1982	0.0	1.00	
1984	13.7	0.69	
1986	16.0	0.79	

Table 6.8 Massachusetts Democratic Incumbents Reelected, Equation Values

Election	t	α	β
Congress			
	1976	53	0.24
	1978	14	0.79
	1980	19	0.61
	1982	37	0.50
	1984	40	0.33
	1986	40	0.57
State Senate			
	1976	44	0.33
	1978	65	0.10
	1980	44	0.37
	1982	33	0.48
	1984	51	0.29
	1986	36	0.50

tional cases, however, and otherwise, the level-specific variables are the better predictors of partisan behavior.

The results are similarly inconclusive regarding the impact of congressional or state senate conditions or gubernatorial voting patterns. In general, accounting for conditions at both the congressional and state senate levels increased the predictive capacity of the simple gubernatorial equations (see appendix). However, in five of the six gubernatorial elections studied, the congressional conditions had a much greater influence on gubernatorial voting than did the state senate conditions. In fact, in three of the elections, state senatorial conditions played no significant role in predicting patterns of voting for governor.

In sum, the extent to which conditions at one electoral level play a role in determining outcomes at other levels is debatable. Although indications point to the presence of some interlevel coattail effects, their strength is not consistent enough to draw conclusions about their impact.

The Impact of Redistricting on Voting Behavior

The behavior of Massachusetts and Connecticut indicates that the partisan behavior and profile of a given town or constituency are indeed affected by the conditions under which voting occurs. Voters are more likely to behave consistently when stable, familiar conditions endure. Yet even under similar conditions (the reelection of a sitting incumbent, for example), voters do not necessarily behave in a consistent partisan manner.

In the congressional and state senatorial districts in both states, in which the Democratic incumbent was reelected, there were marked shifts from year to year in the partisan bias and the propensity to vote Democratic, despite the fact that the districts remained Democratic and reelected the same candidate (see tables 6.7 and 6.8). Even when the political environment is stable (that is, the incumbents are reelected), the propensity to vote for one party or the other varies markedly. Whether this variability is a function of the changing quality of challengers, the absence of challengers, or external factors such as a presidential election is less important than the fact that the variability occurs and that it is constant. This marked variation indicates that shorthand measures of statewide partisanship such as seats-votes ratios and base-race standards are unsuited for the purpose of determining fair representation in a district system.

This analysis indicates that partisanship is not necessarily constant and that changes in districts and candidates can cause marked changes in the partisan behavior of a constituency. Furthermore, statewide measures of partisan swing tell us little about the partisan behavior of a given constituency, since political conditions and candidates are not the same statewide. Thus, any analysis of redistricting's impact, and any claim that a particular districting scheme is indeed a gerrymander, must account for the changing political conditions under which voting takes place, to determine if a given constituency has been denied its fair representation.

Of course, Massachusetts and Connecticut are but two of fifty states; their behavior is not necessarily typical of other states or of the country as a whole. Nonetheless, we can draw some general conclusions about the implications of this analysis for the study of voting behavior, representation, and the impact of gerrymandering on both.

7

Conclusion: Political Science, Representation, and Politics

The results of this study suggest that the political and legal conceptualization of fair representation and the attempts to ensure the opportunity for it require reassessment and further study. Theories of representation and the arguments upon which gerrymandering analyses are based simply do not reflect the realities of partisan electoral behavior. As a result, the redistricting process—along with the studies of it by political and legal scholars—is riddled with internal contradictions and inconsistencies that are nurtured by the flaws in the prevailing paradigm of political science analysis. Furthermore, the remedies proposed by these scholars and the means by which the courts order their implementation now appear to be impotent because the principal cure (that is, remedial redistricting) for unfair representation is prescribed on the basis of inaccurate observations of partisan electoral behavior.

At the outset, a definition of gerrymandering was set forth, asserting that denial of representational opportunity must be the central aspect of gerrymandering analysis and the sine qua non of any gerrymandering claim. If redistricting were not perceived as a threat to the fair representation of political groups, gerrymandering itself would be of little concern. The analysis in chapters 4, 5, and 6 indicates that the gerrymandering controversy requires much more study, because denial of partisan representational opportunity is difficult to define—let alone to prove or remedy. Logic dictates that in order to be denied its representational opportunity, a constituency must be clearly a member of one partisan camp or another. In the same way that a racially heterogeneous constituency cannot be denied its opportunity to be represented as black or white or Asian or Hispanic, and so forth, a constituency that is not consistently Democratic or Republican cannot be said to have been denied its fair opportunity to be represented as one or the other. Similarly, for a party to cry gerrymander, it must be able to prove that such staunch partisan constituencies exist and that the district plan actually dilutes the party's support by causing such constituencies' votes to be wasted.

The variability of the partisan behavior of the towns in this analysis indicates the difficulty in labeling constituencies as consistently partisan. In fact, their behavior substantiates V. O. Key's assertions about secular realignments and the fluidity of partisan behavior: "Put baldly, the thesis might be, place a person of specified characteristics in a specified status in the social system and he forthwith becomes a Democrat (or Republican)."[1] If constituencies can be Democratic in one district and Republican in another, if they can be Democratic while their incumbent is in office and Republican after the incumbent retires, then they cannot be labeled partisan in the sense that their representation depends on one party or the other's holding a certain percentage of the seats in a legislature. Of course, this analysis has sought only to highlight the volatility that can occur in partisan behavior; it does not suggest that Democratic or Republican strongholds are nonexistent. It serves, however, to expose the weakness of the assumption that Democrats in different parts of a state are always comparable or that votes for the Republican party's candidates always have the same meaning.

If, in a given election or districting scheme, one party's percentage of the seats is significantly smaller than its percentage of the vote, the claim by party leaders of unfairness or gerrymandering may be legitimate. But resolution seems to require the parties to find more attractive candidates, instead of or in addition to seeking to reshuffle voters—who, when given the opportunity to vote for different candidates, are not unlikely to change their partisan behavior. Although such a situation may be described accurately as underrepresentation of the party-in-the-government, this analysis has shown that it may not easily be described as denial of representational opportunity of the party-in-the-electorate.

Naturally, some constituencies can be labeled Democratic or Republican. If town X always supports one party by a lopsided margin, regardless of who the candidates are or how many contest a given election, we could conclude that such a town or city is firmly in the camp of the party that receives a majority of its votes. Such categorization becomes much more difficult, however, when towns such as those in Heckler's district or those moved from Boland's to Conte's behave in a much less consistent manner. Since the towns analyzed appeared to be in a process of partisan transition, they would have been hard to characterize accurately. Heckler's Republican constituents, for example, certainly did not live up to the expectations of the Massachusetts Democratic party leadership, who had expected them to continue to support Heckler when she ran against Frank. Clearly, representing the same constituency in different elections or under different conditions can mean different things.

The concept of representation and the denial of fair representational opportunity make sense, therefore, only when certain unrealistic assumptions are made about voting behavior and the nature of political groups: first, that the group in question meets some criteria of cohesion and durability from election to election, that is, the group is identifiable; second, that the group in question is durable and cohesive and the group's size and representational entitlement are measurable; and third, that voters are *party* voters. That is, a Democratic vote in one district will be a Democratic vote in another, regardless of the candidates, and party votes in one part of a state are equatable with party votes in other parts. Accordingly, the party-in-the-government and the party-in-the-electorate must be regarded as cohesive entities.

Key and Burnham, among others, have questioned the legitimacy of such assumptions (see chapter 3, above). As shown by the marked partisan changes that occur when incumbents retire or towns are redistricted, the tie a voter feels to the legislature may be as much a function of the appeal of the candidate as of the party label the candidate bears.

The durability of partisan sentiment and the periodic upheaval of partisan political cleavages are central aspects of electoral research. Discussions of such changes are predicated on the belief that durable partisan blocs of voters exist and that a large-scale political crisis is necessary to realign them. The fluctuations in the behavior of the towns in this study indicate that an analysis based on this approach is bound to be inaccurate.

The shifts that occur in response to changes in the electoral environment reinforce Burnham's contention that politics means different things to different people at different times.[2] Clearly, politics sometimes means different things to different people in different districts or even when confronted by new electoral choices in the same district. The amount of fluctuation that occurs over time—even in those districts where incumbent candidates win year after year—lends more credence to Key's theory of secular realignment than the theory of critical elections.[3] Partisan blocs are much less durable than critical elections theories suggest; in fact these blocs appear to be in a constant state of flux.

Theories that attempt to force voters into clear-cut partisan categories, despite the fact that their behavior manifests significantly nonpartisan, candidate-oriented tendencies, are appealing in their simplicity but do not accurately reflect reality. Granted, political theories can more easily be built on assertions such as, Voters are not fools, or Politics means different things to different people at different times, than on the assumptions of partisan consistency and the durability of partisan blocs. Nonetheless, the realities of voting behavior seem unlikely to alter to accommodate the niceties of representation theory. Accordingly, political science bears a responsibility to reform its paradigm to accommodate reality.

This analysis has both practical and theoretical implications. The former address the usefulness of political science research in the areas of representation and electoral systems and the capacity of the judiciary to serve as arbitrator of redistricting disputes. So long as political scientists continue to construct measures of partisanship that ignore the realities of voting behavior, the conclusions that can be drawn will be qualified at best. In addition, problems of the political science paradigm notwithstanding, the limits of the judicial process prevent the judiciary from achieving the desired goal of representational fairness. This is so for two reasons. First, the Supreme Court has thus far been unable to construct a coherent theory of group representation or a clear definition of political group. Second, and perhaps more important, the Court has no way of ensuring that the electoral result of a presumed fair redistricting plan will ensure fair representation, even if it had a coherent theory and definition to work with. The theoretical implications address the shortcomings of the political and legal theories of representation upon which gerrymandering analysis is based. As well, they require the reconsideration of how we think about politics and political behavior. Below, I consider the partisan gerrymandering myth and some of its mythical solutions. These solutions are weakened by the theoretical oversights discussed, and thus such antigerrymandering measures are ill-suited for the task of ensuring fair representational opportunity.

New or Improved Measures of Partisanship

Prevailing measures of partisan fairness are conceptually flawed. Seats-votes and swing ratios are grounded on inaccurate assumptions about partisan behavior and are, therefore, of little practical use in determining the inherent fairness of a district plan. Such measures are helpful when applied to a static set of political circumstances, but when conditions change they are no longer applicable.

Some critics have argued that such measures nonetheless serve a valuable purpose, because they provide a starting point for drafting district plans in an unbiased manner.[4] Attempting to use such partisan measures effectively gets the redistricter off the hook, because seats-votes ratios and the like are naturally designed to provide an unbiased reading of a state's partisan pulse. As Howard Scarrow has noted, "What happens after that, when actual legislative elections are held and when many voters may desert their basic party preferences because of a popular candidate, a well-run local campaign or local issue, should not concern us" (ibid. 821). This view, however, overlooks the theoretical basis for embarking on the endeavor to ensure partisan fairness in the redistricting process. If we employ measures of partisan fairness that we know will become inapplicable and that are based on faulty assumptions, we cannot claim that we are ensuring anyone's fair representational opportunity; we are merely manufacturing placebos.

Solutions to the problem of representational denial that would employ registration data or some sort of base race in order to get a better picture of a constituency's partisan divisions actually serve to undermine the representative function of specific elections by diluting or buffering the power of voters to decide contests. Democratic representation requires the active participation of those who are to be represented. If partisans do not participate in elections in a manner that indicates or upholds their partisan beliefs or political agenda, they risk the underrepresentation, or even nonrepresentation, of those beliefs. However, for the gerrymandering analyst to bypass the results of the electoral process and employ other measures of partisanship in order to get a better, more accurate, or simply more easily measured partisan count is as undemocratic as stuffing ballot boxes on behalf of the voters who fail to turn out or fail to vote for the party they are registered or affiliated with.

Base-race measures and seats-votes or swing ratios serve ultimately to disregard the will of the voters as expressed by the electoral institution designed specifically to express it. If the Republicans, who make up a majority of the registrants in town X, fail to turn out and, as a result, a Democratic candidate wins, would we be willing to categorize the town as Republican, simply because our base-race measure differs with the polls? Would we be willing to give the statewide minority party a few extra seats because a seats-votes or swing ratio suggests that it is underrepresented?

The usefulness of such measures of partisanship ends where the supremacy of popular sovereignty begins. Unless gerrymandering analysts wish to employ their measures as a corrective trump on the results of the electoral process, their criticisms and complaints about gerrymandering are rendered moot. If the voters do not behave in an ideal partisan manner, why should their behavior be qualified by the ex post facto employment of an ideal standard?

If political scientists are to give a partisan label to an electorate or its divers constituencies while maintaining the supremacy of popular sovereignty, then they must use actual electoral results. Thus, before gerrymandering analysts contend that a party has been unfairly districted out of power, they must first establish a means by which variable electoral results can be used to produce consistent measures of constituency partisanship.

Voting Systems

One frequently proposed solution to the gerrymandering controversy and the problems it poses for representation theory is a change from a district system to some form of proportional representation.[5] Although the single-member district system cannot be proved to be unfair until gerrymandering theory's terms are better defined, proportional representation poses a solution to representation problems insofar as it removes the sources of the claims of unfairness—the districts themselves.

As long as mathematical standards are employed to measure the fairness of a given system of voting, single-member district systems will always be regarded unfavorably, for the simple reason that they are intended *not* to produce proportional results. Insofar as the disproportionality of SMP systems is designed to produce a clear winner of an election—thereby avoiding the problems of postelection government formation inherent to PR systems—SMP serves a valuable purpose. The question remains, Is the certainty of outcomes and the stability of an SMP system worth the disproportional results that the system tends to produce?

Although a transition to proportional representation might provide mathematically fairer election results, it would not necessarily settle questions of representational opportunity. Whereas the American SMP system of voting and candidate selection is decentralized, the proportional representation alternative is not. The American district system, replete with open, direct primaries, provides a maximization of opportunities for popular control not only of general election results but also of the nature of the candidate choice offered in the general election. In most PR systems however, candidate selection is in large part the responsibility of the party leadership. Determining which party members are on the list of candidates submitted for a give election, as well as the order in which the candidates appear on the ballot, is seldom determined by the voters.[6]

Whether or not a transition to proportional representation would provide a qualitatively better form of representation is therefore debatable. Under a PR system, popular candidates who were not in good standing with party leaders would be unlikely to hold a favorable position on the party list and, therefore, less likely to hold a legislative seat; an SMP system, such as that employed in the United States, might allow them to run in a direct primary. In the extreme case, the party leadership would be in a position literally to shut out candidates who represent the party fringe. Under such conditions, parties would be more certain to receive a fair allotment of legislative seats in an assembly, but the extent to which they actually represented the opinions of the voters who voted for the party would be subject to question.

The question of which system is inherently better remains a topic for debate. The arguments for PR systems and single-member district systems are both well substantiated, and they are fundamentally at odds with one another. Although these arguments are elaborated at length elsewhere,[7] one alternative system deserves special mention as a possible means of reconciling the issues in the current American gerrymandering controversy.

The Limited Vote: A Possible Middle Ground

The American gerrymandering controversy is fueled fundamentally by two competing desires: to maintain our district system of representation, which defines constituencies geographically, and to give other constituencies and groups for which geographically designed systems of voting are not ideal a chance to be represented.[8] Currently, for example, states are required by the amended Voting Rights Act to draw district lines in a manner that will permit selected geographically dispersed racial minorities the opportunity to vote as a majority in a given legislative or congressional district. The result of such measures is district plans that are highly controversial because of their contorted boundaries.[9] One congressional district in particular (the North Carolina First District) is so contorted that "two of its parts appear to be connected by a river, with the banks on each side in other districts" (ibid.).

A resolution to the tension between ensuring group representational opportunity and preserving geographically relevant district lines might employ multi-member districts with limited-vote mechanisms. Although such schemes are usually recommended for enhancing minority voting power,[10] they would (at least in theory) present one means of defusing partisan representation disputes as well. In a system of limited voting, more than one representative serves a given district. However, the voters are not permitted to vote for all the representatives. By giving voters fewer votes than there are seats to be filled in the district, a limited vote system forces partisans to vote strategically in order to maximize the chances of electing their preferred candidates.

Regarding racially polarized areas, group definition is a reasonably straightforward endeavor. Despite the fact that this analysis has indicated that partisan group definition is difficult (if not impossible), the goal of ensuring to whatever partisan groups exist an opportunity to cohere and elect a preferred candidate would be attained, at least formally. If voters are in fact staunch partisans, the limited-vote system would place the burden on them to vote strategically and, as a cohesive group, elect one of their own. If voters are not such partisans, they would continue to vote in the volatile manner displayed in this study, regardless of the opportunities provided by the voting scheme. Accordingly, such a voting arrangement would, at least in form, remove a key ground for claims of partisan gerrymandering, since it would, by design, provide opportunities for group representation.

The Rights of Legislators and Political Parties

If we step away from the quagmire of trying to determine fair representation of parties-in-the-electorate, one burning questions remains: What are the rights of the candidates? If an incumbent loses after a redistricting, can we prove that the changes that occurred in the composition of his or her district were the cause of defeat? Although our sense of fair play might lead us at first to concede a losing incumbent's right to redress, the practicalities of such a situation will cause us to reconsider. First, any such claim would necessarily have to be predicated on proof that the redistricting caused the candidate to lose. Such proof might well be impossible.

How, for example, would we resolve a situation such as occurred in Massachusetts in 1982? Since the new district plan was drawn by Democrats to purge one of their own (Barney Frank), it was not regarded as a gerrymander in the partisan sense of the word: true gerrymanders seem to require conflict between parties, not within them. But, since this attempted gerrymander backfired, could Heckler claim that she had been mistreated? If the gerrymander had knocked Frank out of office, would he or his constituents have had some grounds for redress?

A similar problem hampers attempts to prove that representational opportunity has been denied to a group of voters. If a 65 percent Democratic constituency is moved into a competitive Republican district and, despite the fact that the constituency slips to only 45 percent Democratic, the additional Democratic votes still cause the district to go Democratic in the ensuing election, can we say that gerrymandering—the denial of representational opportunity—has been inflicted on the Republican party's supporters?

In situations where states lose congressional districts—such as that which took place in Massachusetts between 1980 and 1982—gerrymandering seems harder to prove or remedy, because someone is bound to lose representation, since the size of a state's congressional delegation must be reduced. It is a much more serious issue, however, when states gain seats. If a state gains or at least does not lose representation in Congress, it seems unlikely that the minority party should experience seat loss as a result of redistricting. Its percentage of the delegation may drop, but it would be surprising if its raw number of seats decreased. This type of minority-party seat loss actually occurred in California in 1980–82. The redistricting plan drafted by the state legislature's Democratic majority forced several Republican incumbents to run against each other in collapsed districts.[11] Can this ravaging of minority party incumbents be justified?

The answer to this question derives from our perception of the relationship between the party-in-the-government and the voters. If the party labels actually are the principal determinants of voting behavior, then the predatory ravaging of incumbents in this way could certainly be seen as an abridgment of the representational opportunity of the minority party's voters. But, since party does not seem to be the principal determinant of partisan behavior, the sacking of incumbents in this manner cannot necessarily be regarded as an outright denial of representation to the voters.

When we shift the focus of the gerrymandering discussion from the party-in-the-electorate to the party-in-the-government, the issues at stake are those of intraparty democracy and the rights of majority and minority parties in legislatures. If a party can censure a member, can it not seek to get rid of him by other means—such as redistricting him out of office? Wouldn't such a censure abridge the representational opportunity of the ousted congressman's supporters? On the other hand, if a majority can assert its will against a minority on any other piece of legislation, why should its authority be restricted when the legislation involves the drawing of district lines?

The question of the rights of legislators and parties has been addressed only cursorily in court cases that addressed specific aspects of the legislative process and party organization.[12] Since such rights are not even mentioned in the Constitution, the disposition of conflicts concerning them remains unclear. Not a few of the complaints concerning legislative procedures have been rejected by the Court on grounds that they comprised political questions.[13] Accordingly, it is difficult to discuss the nature of the rights of legislators and parties. Nonetheless, we can discuss the Court's role in adjudicating the representation cases that form the backdrop for such disputes.

Despite the fact that remedial redistricting may actually be self-defeating, the Court's involvement in the redistricting process has been and obviously remains necessary. As shown by the Court's involvement in racial gerrymandering cases and voting rights cases, there are times when clear situations of electoral discrimination arise and legal intervention may be the only means of remedying the unfair situation. The question remains: What role can or should the courts assume?

The Role of the Courts

Despite Justice White's contention in *Davis v. Bandemer* that questions of fairness do indeed fall within the purview of the equal protection clause of the Fourteenth Amendment, O'Connor's assertions in that case about the mutability of partisanship and Rutledge's assertions about the want of equity in *Colegrove v. Green* are substantiated by this analysis. The variability of partisan behavior prevents us from clearly identifying who the plaintiff group is in a partisan gerrymandering dispute. Without a clearly recognizable plaintiff, the Court is unable to determine the extent to which a particular right has been denied, and therefore, it is unable to prescribe an adequate remedy. With regard to a partisan gerrymandering dispute, the representability of the plaintiff group depends upon our ability to measure its size and then determine its fair representation. Since, as this analysis has shown, the Court and political science are unable to do this, the justification for the Court's entrance into the political thicket of gerrymandering is questionable.

Assuming that the Court could justify its involvement on the basis of White's Fourteenth Amendment arguments, questions remain: Does the Court's performance in this area justify its continued involvement, in light of O'Connor's and Rutledge's concerns about want of equity? Is the Court any better equipped than political scientists to analyze electoral returns? Can a coherent case law of representation be established?

The Court cannot mandate that an election will produce a fair representational result, even if the election occurs in the most meticulously and fairly drawn districts. Ultimately, the assurance of fair representation is dependant upon the partisan behavior of voters—the regulation of which is certainly beyond the scope of judicial authority. Judicial involvement in redistricting disputes ultimately exacerbates political tensions and damages the authority and legitimacy of the judiciary by exposing its weaknesses. Can the judiciary justify its participation in a particular dispute if it is incapable of resolving it?

In *The Courts and Social Policy,* for example, Donald Horowitz questions the Court's capacity and ability to resolve a range of issues of social policy that lend themselves better to resolution by legislative bargaining and deliberation.[14] As he explains, questions of capacity focus "not on whether the Courts *should* perform certain tasks but on whether they *can* perform them competently" (18, emphasis in original). Furthermore, he continues, "where episodic intervention [by the courts] would not be enough [to resolve a given dispute], that is a sign that there is no judicial question present" (293). Analysts of judicial capacity such as Horowitz are thus particularly concerned with the quality of the results (that is, the impact) of judicial decisions, because this is the one aspect of the judicial process over which the Court has no control.

Even when the Supreme Court has the opportunity to repair a particular lower court or previous decision, it is invariably hampered by the limits placed on its ability to collect information about the case. Since an appealed case is framed in specific terms, the Court is unable to venture beyond the bounds of a dispute as it is framed by the parties to the case. As a result, the Court is forced to make narrow, perhaps belated, decisions. Says Horowitz: "as the judicial process neglects social facts in favor of historical facts, so, too does it slight what might be called *consequential facts.* Judges base their decisions on *antecedent facts,* on behavior that antedates the litigation" (51, emphasis in original). Since courts cannot be certain that a decision based on historical facts will apply well to present or future situations, they cannot anticipate reactions to their decisions or be certain that their decision will be appropriate.

Redistricting disputes are clearly based upon what Horowitz refers to as historical facts. Since we cannot be certain of how voters will react when their political environment changes, we can categorize them—either individually or as they are grouped into constituencies—*only* on the basis of their previous partisan behavior. But since previous partisan behavior under one set of electoral circumstances does not necessarily indicate future partisan behavior under a different set, a judicial decision to alter a districting plan on the basis of prior electoral behavior is, to a significant degree, little more than guesswork. Furthermore, if a court mandates the creation of a new "fair" map which, nonetheless, fails to achieve the desired partisan result, it can do nothing to repair the map again until a new plaintiff brings a case.

Of course, one might argue that some sort of affirmative action policy is required to ensure fairness of representational opportunity. Judicially appointed agents could oversee the drafting of districting plans to ensure that new maps do not disadvantage particular partisan groups. The results of this analysis indicate, however, that the judiciary cannot seek to ensure outcomes in representation disputes in the same way that it did, for example, in response to the resistance to school desegregation orders. Whereas its affirmative action decisions could be enforced by means as extreme as those used by Presidents Kennedy and Eisenhower when they mobilized militia in support of desegregation orders, the Court cannot require voters to vote in a particular manner to ensure that specific numbers of party candidates are elected.

Popular or institutional resistance to some Supreme Court decisions can thus be overcome. However, the barriers to the effective implementation of partisan redistricting decisions cannot be overcome, because they arise not from political resistance but from the fickle nature of voters. Even if every redistricter in the country agreed to abide by some judicially sanctioned abstract standard of fairness when drawing maps, the Court would still be unable to ensure fair representation of political groups, because it cannot force voters to vote at all, let alone to behave in a consistent partisan manner.

The Court has now expounded principles of fair representation and districting that do not apply to an electorate characterized by shifting partisan loyalties. The Court's perception of voting and partisanship may make sense in theory but not in practice. Therefore, we must question its involvement in such cases. In *Baker v. Carr,* Justice Frankfurter chastised the other justices for getting involved in a matter (reapportionment) that lent itself to such theorizing: a "hypothetical claim resting on abstract assumptions is now for the first time made the basis for affording illusory relief for a particular evil even though it foreshadows deeper and more pervasive difficulties in consequence" (267).

If, as Horowitz contends, the judiciary's inability to resolve a given problem suggests that there may not be a constitutional question, we must ask what benefit is derived from the judicial exposition of abstract standards of fairness to hypothetical electorates. Should the courts continue to engage in a dispute that they cannot resolve? Can they legitimately do so? If, by deciding that certain redistricting plans are unfair, the Court causes a legislature to expend more time and resources in order to create hypothetically improved district maps, it seems likely that, sooner or later, it will begin to incur that legislature's, and the public's, resentment. Frankfurter himself asserted this in *Baker:*

> Disregard of inherent limits in the effective exercise of the Court's "judicial Power" not only presages the futility of judicial intervention in the essentially political conflict of forces by which the relation between population and representation has time out of mind been and now is determined. It may well impair the Court's position as the ultimate organ of "the supreme Law of the Land" in that vast range of legal problems, often strongly entangled in popular feeling, on which this Court must pronounce. The Court's authority—possessed of neither the purse nor the sword—ultimately rests on sustained public confidence in its moral sanction. Such feeling must be nourished by the Court's complete detachment, in fact and in appearance, from political entanglements and by abstention from injecting itself into the clash of political forces in political settlements. (267)

Although Frankfurter was concerned primarily with the political questions of reapportionment disputes, his rationale and arguments for judicial retreat apply as well to questions of judicial impact in partisan representation and gerrymandering cases. Setting forth decisions that cannot produce the Court's desired outcome of fair representational opportunity certainly meets Frankfurter's and Horowitz's criteria for overstepping the bounds of judicial legitimacy.

If, as Frankfurter contended in his dissent in *Baker,* "to promulgate jurisdiction in the abstract is meaningless" (268), we must now ask if the courts should not reconsider the wisdom of their involvement in partisan redistricting cases. Supreme Court decisions have served only to create a line of increasingly murky precedents that provide a weak foundation of case law. To the extent that "the [Supreme] Court, like other institutions, is in part the maker of the tradition that influences it,"[15] the Court has trapped itself within the political thicket of representation issues.

As a result of the Supreme Court's inability to formulate a coherent theory of representation, the lower courts have been at a loss to abide by its decisions. A good example of the Supreme Court's exacerbation of the difficulties inherent in the adjudication of redistricting cases occurred in the circuit court case, *Kirksey v. Board of Supervisors of Hinds County.* In this case, the Fifth Circuit Court struck down a county redistricting plan on the grounds that it denied minority access to the political process. In a concurring opinion, Judge Gee expressed his frustration with the criteria for determining unfair representation practices set forth by the Supreme Court in *United Jewish Organizations of Williamsburg v. Carey,* where the Court allowed the division of a Hasidic community to permit consolidation of a black majority. "The clear implication of *United Jewish Organizations* is that a life-tenured magistrate is to exercise a casting vote in the selection of local legislators. For who does not know that by judicious tinkering with apportioning lines, almost any electoral outcome desired can be produced? . . . What seems to be envisioned is something more approximating a tribal council than a representative body chosen by republican methods" (*Kirksey,* 156).

Although Judge Gee's faith in the predictability of redistricting-induced electoral outcomes is undermined by the analysis in this work, his frustration with the signals sent out by the Supreme Court is clear. Despite his serious disagreement with the Court's attempts to set forth a coherent definition of discriminatory districting, he ultimately decided simply to abide by the Court's desires, regardless of whether or not they made sense.

Doubtless the Court holds a coherent vision of better things to come which is denied me. At any rate, I am sustained by the recollection that it is not for us to pursue matters of national policy in competition with or obstruction of the Court. Where relevant precedent exists, our duty is to ascertain and obey that which is closest and most recent. For the time being, that is *United Jewish Organizations.* Since it is, I

> concur in the en banc court's judgment invalidating those of our panel and the district court, though not in its opinion. (ibid., 156–57)

Of course, the opinion of one frustrated circuit court judge does not represent a wholesale condemnation of the Supreme Court's attempts to decide representation cases. However, it indicates that the confusion outlined in chapter 2 above has served only to create more confusion as the courts have continued to attempt to resolve representation disputes without sufficiently studying electoral change. Since the adjudicatory process prevents them from doing so, the courts are bound to continue making poor and ineffectual decisions, which result only in frustration such as Judge Gee's and resistance by state legislatures.

The wisest route for the judiciary would be to limit its involvement to those areas of the electoral process in which it can operate effectively and make decisions under the auspices of a constitutional referent. The constitutionally sanctioned equality of district populations and access to the ballot box can be derived easily from the Fourteenth and Fifteenth Amendments. Furthermore, it is fairly easy to check to see if states or municipalities are complying with a judicial decree on such matters. It is beyond the ability or capacity of the courts or political scientists to ensure particular electoral outcomes, no matter how fair the representational opportunity of the competing groups seems to be. No matter how meticulous we are in our cartography, gerrymanders and remedial redistricting plans can fail—and fail miserably—simply because the voters are always free to change their minds.

Representation Theory and Gerrymandering

The conclusions drawn by this work regarding partisan behavior undermine the premises upon which prevailing conceptions of representative government and the relationship between the representative and the represented constituency are based. Representation theory presupposes fundamentally that representatives are in fact capable of identifying and describing the members of their constituencies and their interests; if this is not the case, they can hardly claim to be representatives. As a result of this assumption, political scientists, legal scholars, and gerrymandering analysts have focused on the behavior of the *representative*—as opposed to the *represented*—and propagated corollaries about the nature of the representational relationship between the party-in-the-electorate and the party-in-the-government.

This aspect of representation theory focuses on the mandate-independence controversy, which addresses exclusively the role of the representative because (it assumes) the nature and interests of the represented are obvious. As Hannah Pitkin states in her treatise on representation, the mandate-independence controversy revolves around the following question: "Should (must) a representative do what his constituents want, and be bound by mandates or instructions from them; or should (must) he be free to act as seems best to him in pursuit of their welfare?"[16] In response, Pitkin later answers that representation in the political sense means

> acting in the interest of the represented, in a manner responsive to them. The representative must act independently; his action must involve discretion and judgment; he must be the one who acts. The *represented* must also be (*conceived as*) capable of independent action and judgment, not merely being taken care of. And, despite the resulting potential for conflict between the representative and the represented about what is to be done, that conflict must not normally take place. The representative must act in such a way that there is no conflict, or if it occurs an explanation is called for. He must not be found persistently at odds with the wishes of the represented without good reason in terms of their interest, without a good explanation of why their wishes are not in accord with their interest. (209–10, emphasis added)

The two most telling words in this passage are "conceived as." As Pitkin shows, theories of political representation presuppose the existence of a consistent, cohesive, and well-defined constituent interest. That is, when a representative is given cause to explain himself or to speak out on some issue, it will be perfectly clear why he must, to whom he is responsible, and for whom he speaks. Although this may seem intuitively reasonable under ideal theoretical conditions, it is unlikely in practice, because the partisan profile and partisan loyalty of a constituency are by no means constant.

As we have seen, this is so because constituencies are composed of numerous, distinct individuals, who are not necessarily diehard partisans or participants in elections. Thus, a change in one or more voters' perception of interest can cause a corresponding change in the constituency's expression of interest. This only exacerbates the problem of representation, by upsetting the simplicity of the most basic element of representation theory's paradigm: the designation of one agent by one principal. Theoretically, the agent in this situation understands clearly the instructions and interests of the principal. Thus, in the legislature, the agent is able to express the principal's instructions clearly or use his own discretion to further the principal's welfare if the opportunity to achieve the principal's instructed goals does not arise.

This idealization presupposes that the principal's interests are constant and independent of the choice of agent. In reality, however, the expression of the principal's interests may be conditioned by his perception of the agent, as well as the number and quality of the agents from which he may choose. As the behavior of Massachusetts and Connecticut towns indicates, this is certainly true with regard to the electoral expression of partisan interest. Furthermore, since popularly elected agents are chosen by plural principals, it is questionable whether any elected official can claim that he is able to represent accurately and adequately the interest of a constituency. How can one representative be 40 percent Democratic, 30 percent Republican, 15 percent independent, and 15 percent nonvoting at the same time?

The representative can be said to have three possible partisan constituencies: (1) those loyal partisans who always vote for him, regardless of whether or not he is challenged, (2) those who turn out for him only when he is challenged, and (3) the entire district. To what extent can the best interests and opinions of his district be divined if the incumbent's margin of victory varies from year to year? Is his power stronger when he wins big in a low turnout election or when he wins a closely contested race with a high rate of voter participation? Unless political theory can decide which of these three choices is the proper definition of *constituency,* it will be impossible to determine who is supposed to be represented and who is not.

Clearly, the nature of both the mandate sent by the towns in this study and their general welfare changed significantly from one election to the next, despite the fact that the same incumbent and party won several of the elections. This would seem to require the representative to redefine his or her job after each election. Should the representative act in a more partisan manner because he wins an uncontested race? What should the representative do when more voters participate in a contested election but a smaller percentage vote for him because the other party runs a candidate? The answers to and implications of these questions depend upon how we regard the behavior of the electorate. Thus, Pitkin's question should be rephrased to read not What does/should a representative do? but instead For whom does he do it, and how does he know what to do?

Furthermore, this conceptualization overlooks the fact that the representative-constituency relationship is not necessarily comparable to the relationship between the party-in-the-government and the party-in-the-electorate. Whereas the former comprises one member of the party and a specific (albeit plural) constituency, the latter includes several of both. Although the elected representatives may all bear the party label, the divers constituencies see the party as represented by different individuals. As a result, the party may be more or less attractive depending on the persona of its candidates. Correspondingly, constituents will be more or less likely to vote for the party depending on who the party nominates in their district.

Once we determine or can agree upon the proper mandate-independence balance of roles for a representative, the questions still remain: To whom (that is, to what constituency) is the representative beholden? Is the representative responsible to all constituents or only to those who voted for him? If the number of voters who support or oppose him in a given election changes, does the nature of his representational relationship change as well? If so, how?

The dearth of clear answers to such questions suggests that the term *repre-

sentative government may be a misnomer. What makes a government representative? To the extent that a government is popularly elected, we can say that it is accountable to the people. But the opportunity for the populace to recall a legislator—or at least to "throw the rascal out"—is not tantamount to the assurance that the casting of a vote ensures the manifestation of interests or achievement of desired policy goals in a legislature. To hypothesize that voters—if they choose to vote—vote for the candidate who most closely approximates their own interests does not necessarily imply that the voters regard the choices as good ones. As Pitkin notes: "Perhaps representation must be redefined to fit our politics; perhaps we must simply accept the fact that what we have been calling representative government is in reality just party competition for office" (221).

In this context, attempts to prevent and remedy partisan gerrymandering as a means of ensuring fair representation put the cart before the horse. Gerrymandering cannot be a threat to representation if we have yet to determine exactly what we mean by partisan representation. If we are to determine with clarity the meaning of representation—let alone the concept of its denial by gerrymander—we must shift our focus of analysis from the fate of the party-in-the-government to the behavior of the party-in-the-electorate, because we must first decide and define what it means to represent an electorate composed of voters who do not always vote—and when they do vote, do not do so in a consistent partisan manner.

This is no simple task, because the concept of representation suggests a consistency of constituent interest not manifested by the partisan behavior of voters. A district may certainly be urban or rural, industrial or agricultural, ethnically homogenous or heterogeneous; but if the split of the partisan vote differs from the other existing political cleavages, representation theory is at a loss to tell us whether we should represent the constituency's expressed interest or its unexpressed, but nonetheless extant, interest, which is reflected in its ethnic, economic, or geographic traits. Perhaps the ideal relation between the party-in-the-electorate and the party-in-the-government is not attainable in an electorate characterized by fluid partisan loyalties. If this is the case, political scientists must reformulate their theories of partisanship, representation, and gerrymandering or risk irrelevance.

Summary

Those trying to explain the reapportionment-redistricting puzzle have operated under incorrect theoretical assumptions and have failed thus far to come to grips with the implications of the political data that clearly undermine these assumptions. Gerrymandering analysis has been based upon theories of representation that presuppose the existence of well-ordered and consistent voter preferences. This analysis of voters in Massachusetts and Connecticut indicates that voters are consistent neither in their partisan behavior nor their likelihood to vote in a given election. These analysts have been ill-equipped for the task of stalking the gerrymander. Whereas the courts and political scientists have entered other political thickets with at least some conception of what their prey looked like,[17] they have no real clue about the gerrymander, because they have not paid attention to the inconclusive nature of studies of voting behavior.

Perhaps we seek to protect an ideal type of voter, one who is a well-informed, eager participant who can look toward well-organized, disciplined, and ideologically distinct political parties, whose candidates bear the party label only because they uphold the party's ideology. Unfortunately, neither the voters nor the parties approximate such ideal types, and the reasons and explanations as to why have been well documented (see chapter 3 and accompanying notes). The implications of the contradictions and incorrect analyses that currently characterize the study of representation and gerrymandering extend farther than the bounds of political science treatises. How we view politics and political behavior in a democracy is conditioned in large part by the political observers who explain it to us and theorize about it.

As currently cast, gerrymandering is a threat to anyone who can be regarded as a member of a political group—which means everyone. My analysis suggests that this conclusion not only is mistaken but also enhances group divisiveness since it portrays redistricting as a zero-sum game among groups. Certainly, it is accurate to describe redistricting in zero-sum terms when referring to racially torn areas, but in many instances, such a depiction is wrong and inaccurate. Since political science qua the science of politics purports to study and explain politics for the benefit of all concerned, the discipline would seem to bear the responsibility for addressing the paradigmatic flaws that have surfaced as a result of the gerrymandering issue and that now plague attempts to resolve it.

In his recent work, *Liberal Democracy and Political Science,* James Ceaser notes that the role and relevance of political science in a liberal democracy depends, among other things, upon the accuracy of its observations. "Political science, as an enterprise in society, has a distinct role. It takes the place of a portion of the tutelary power that is assigned to the state in nonliberal regimes. Political science performs this task . . . by inserting itself into society on the strength of an appeal to reason. . . . It aims to influence 'those who direct society'."[18] In light of the obvious yet ignored paradigmatic flaws that political science maintains in its analysis of gerrymandering, it seems that the discipline has lost part of this "appeal to reason." Without a reinvestigation and reanalysis of representation theory, voting, and partisanship, political science will continue to propagate the false reflection of the realities of electoral behavior, which currently forms the foundation for claims of gerrymandering and unfairness. While ensuring further conflict among political groups, this situation will do little to increase our understanding of representation.

Appendix

Table A.1 Connecticut Equations, 1972-1974

uation		F	t-stat	ESS	R-square
gistration					
nple:	D%(1974) = 2.65 + 0.93D%(1972).	2,960		510	0.957
ngress					
nple:	D%(1974) = 39 + 0.34D%(1972).	32		10,209	0.193
mplete:	D%(1974) = 34 + 0.64D%(1972) - 14.6cdem - 20cincr.	24	10.2	5,399	0.573
nate					
nple:	D%(1974) = 18 + 0.84D%(1972).	198		5,408	0.600
mplete:	D%(1974) = 30 + 0.57D%(1972) + 0.42sdiw - 17.4sincd - 12.7sincr.	41	6.6	4,107	0.696

gnificant at $p = 0.05$ level; otherwise significant at the $p = 0.01$ level.

Table A.2 Connecticut Equations, 1974-1976

ation		F	t-stat	ESS	R-square
istration					
ple:	D%(1976) = 2 + 0.95D%(1974).	6,571		214	0.980
gress					
ple:	D%(1976) = 0 + 1.0D%(1974).	156		10,876	0.542
plete:	D%(1976) = 0 + 0.72D%(1974) - 0.1cdiw + 15cdem.	99	21.9	7,230	0.696
ate					
ple:	D%(1976) = 0 + 0.85D%(1974).	224		5,678	0.629
plete:	D%(1976) = 0 + 0.79D%(1974) + 0.04sdiw.*	44	5.45	4,022	0.737

ificant at $p = 0.05$ level; otherwise significant at the $p = 0.01$ level.

Table A.3 Connecticut Equations, 1976-1978

Equation		F	t-stat	ESS	R-squ
Registration					
Simple:	D%(1978) = 0 + 1.01D%(1976).	3,583		417	0
Congress					
Simple:	D%(1978) = 21 + 0.73D%(1976).	388		4,344	0
Complete:	D%(1978) = 13 + 0.79D%(1976) + 0.29crl.*	114	5.55	3,791	0
Senate					
Simple:	D%(1978) = 10 + 0.9D%(1976).	334		4,882	0
Complete:	D%(1978) = 6.5* + 0.95D%(1976) - 0.17sdw + 5sdem.*	67	6.65	4,138	0
Governor					
Simple:	D%(1978) = 24 + 0.59D%(1976).	100		4,382	0
Congress:	D%(1978) = 18 + 0.77D%(1976) - 0.16crl.	36	7.83	3,646	0
Senate:	D%(1978) = 21 + 0.6D%(1976) + 0.11sdiw.	26	5.53	3,457	0

*significant at $p = 0.05$ level; otherwise significant at the $p = 0.01$ level.

Table A.4 Connecticut Equations, 1978-1980

Equation		F	t-stat	ESS	R-sq
Registration					
Simple:	D%(1980) = 0.75 + 0.98D%(1978).	4,417		326	
Congress					
Simple:	D%(1980) = 11 + 0.66D%(1978).	182		6,062	
Complete:	D%(1980) = 29 + 0.8D%(1978) - 0.43cdw - 0.49cdl - 25cincd - 31cincr.	38	3.44	5,266	
Senate					
Simple:	D%(1980) = 5.6* + 0.79D%(1978).	277		5,264	
Complete:	D%(1980) = 0 + 0.78D%(1978) - 0.11sdil - 0.18sdl + 7sdem.	52	4.48	4,182	

*significant at $p = 0.05$ level; otherwise significant at the $p = 0.01$ level.

Table A.5 Connecticut Equations, 1980-1982

Equation	F	t-stat	ESS	R-square
Registration				
Simple: D%(1982) = 0 + 0.99D%(1980).	653		135	0.990
Congress				
Simple: D%(1982) = 0 + 0.85D%(1980).	99		9,557	0.430
Complete: D%(1982) = 0 + 1.15D%(1980) - 0.24cdl.	33	8.42	5,873	0.650
Senate				
Simple: D%(1982) = 0 + 1.03D%(1980).	513		4,385	0.795
Complete: D%(1982) = 0 + 1.38D%(1980) - 0.38sdiw - 0.48sriw - 0.38sdw - 0.49sdl - 0.35srw - 0.54sdr - 0.36srd.	75	3.89	3,342	0.844
Governor				
Simple: D%(1982) = 0 + 0.98D%(1980)	177		5,531	0.573
Congress: D%(1982) = 0 + 1.16D%(1980) - 0.31cdiw* - 14cincr.	34	4.03	4,508	0.652
Senate: D%(1982) = 0 + 0.87D%(1980).	23	---	4,902	0.622

significant at $p = 0.05$ level; otherwise significant at the $p = 0.01$ level.

Table A.6 Connecticut Equations, 1982-1984

Equation	F	t-stat	ESS	R-square
Registration				
Simple: D%(1984) = 0 + 0.96D%(1982).	6,686		198	0.980
Congress				
Simple: D%(1984) = 8 + 0.72D%(1982).	177		6,501	0.574
Complete: D%(1984) = 9 + 0.56D%(1982) + 0.11cdiw + 6cdem.	129	23.2	3,050	0.800
Senate				
Simple: D%(1984) = 4.4 + 0.71D%(1982).	485		2,963	0.786
Complete: D%(1984) = 0 + 0.62D%(1982) + 0.07sdiw* + 13.7sdem + 11.5sincr.*	58		2,655	0.808

significant at $p = 0.05$ level; otherwise significant at the $p = 0.01$ level.

Table A.7 Connecticut Equations, 1984-1986

Equation		F	t-stat	ESS	R-square
Registration					
Simple:	D%(1986) = 0 + 1.02D%(1984).	4,320		322	0.97
Congress					
Simple:	D%(1986) = -19.7 + 1.61D%(1984).	491		9,411	0.78
Complete:	D%(1986) = -9.4 + 1.25D%(1984).	213	13.2	7,511	0.83
Senate					
Simple:	D%(1986) = 0 + 1.4D%(1984).	202		18,098	0.60
Complete:	D%(1986) = 0 + 1.3D%(1984).	36	3.36	15,312	0.66
Governor					
Simple:	D%(1986) = 17 + 0.76D%(1984).	650		1,507	0.83
Congress:	D%(1986) = 17 + 0.74D%(1984).	232	4.52	1,403	0.84
Senate:	D%(1986) = 16 + 0.79D%(1984) - 0.04sriw - 0.04srw.	99	---	1,370	0.84

*significant at $p = 0.05$ level; otherwise significant at the $p = 0.01$ level.

Table A.8 Massachusetts Equations, 1974-1976

Equation		F	t-stat	ESS	R-square
Registration					
Not available.					
Congress					
All towns:					
Simple:	D%(1976) = 7 + 0.83D%(1974).	328		1,107,251	0.495
Complete:	D%(1976) = 40 + 0.24D%(1974) - 0.69criw + 18cdem.	166	110	75,752	0.668
Contested towns (N =303):					
Simple:	D%(1976) = 20 + 0.65D%(1974).	291		64,364	0.491
Complete:	D%(1976) = 18 + 0.24D%(1974) + 35cdem.	116	23.3	49,379	0.610
Senate					
All towns:					
Simple:	D%(1976) = 18 + 0.66D%(1974).	339		1,107,375	0.504
Complete:	D%(1976) = 23 + 0.66D%(1974) - 0.51sriw.	98	8.9	1,018,414	0.543
Contested towns (N = 259):					
Simple:	D%(1976) = 28 + 0.53D%(1974).	170		26,896	0.398
Complete:	D%(1976) = 23 + 0.28D%(1974) + 0.05sdiw + 21sdem.	44	20.1	20,541	0.540

ignificant at $p = 0.05$ level; otherwise significant at the $p = 0.01$ level.

Table A.9 Massachusetts Equations, 1976-1978

Equation		F	t-stat	ESS	R-square
Registration					
Simple:	D%(1978) = 0 + 0.97D%(1976).	7,531		2,938	0.958
Congress					
All towns:					
Simple:	D%(1978) = 0 + 0.89D%(1976).	377		1,591,045	0.53
Complete:	D%(1978) = 31 - 0.97D%(1976) + 1.76cdiw - 17cdem.	841	162	39,392	0.88
Contested towns (N = 216):					
Simple:	D%(1978) = 14 + 0.79D%(1976).	187		34,191	0.46
Complete:	(simple equation = equation for all towns in districts held by Democratic incumbents).				
Senate					
All towns:					
Simple:	D%(1978) = 23 + 0.63D%(1976).	202		1,486,975	0.37
Complete:	D%(1978) = 18 + 0.99D%(1976) - 0.93sdiw - 0.57sriw - 0.98sdw - 1.72sdr + 49sdem.	56	53	69,773	0.70
Contested towns (N = 276):					
Simple:	D%(1978) = 32 + 0.54D%(1976).	148		45,320	0.35
Complete:	D%(1978) = 22 + 0.91D%(1976) - 0.81sdiw - 0.38srw -0.87sdw - 1.33sdr + 43sdem.	83	23	21,998	0.68
Governor					
Simple:	D%(1978) = 5* + 0.76D%(1976).	255		27,776	0.4
Congress:	D%(1978) = 8* + 0.61D%(1976) + 0.26cdiw.	120	25.7	23,494	0.5
Senate:	D%(1978) = 0 + 0.88D%(1976).	41	3.3	26,144	0.4

*significant at $p = 0.05$ level; otherwise significant at the $p = 0.01$ level.

Table A.10 Massachusetts Equations, 1978-1980

uation		F	t-stat	ESS	R-square
gistration					
nple:	D%(1980) = 3.5 + 0.90D%(1978).	3,734		5,644	0.918
ngress					
towns:					
nple:	D%(1980) = 22 + 0.66D%(1978).	1,214		26,879	0.784
mplete:	D%(1980) = 24 + 0.33D%(1978) + 0.28cdiw - 5cdem.*	420	26	20,480	0.835
ntested towns (N = 249):					
nple:	D%(1980) = 15 + 0.63D%(1978).	410		21,862	0.624
mplete:	D%(1980) = 15 + 0.61D%(1978) - 14.5cdem + 18cincd.	210	59	16,135	0.720
nate					
towns:					
nple:	D%(1980) = 7 + 0.83D%(1978).	832		64,178	0.714
mplete:	D%(1980) = 0 + 0.91D%(1978) - 0.32sdiw - 0.4sdw - 0.65sdl + 24sdem.	185	13.5	51,147	0.771
ntested towns (N = 285):					
nple:	D%(1980) = 10 + 0.81D%(1978).	388		34,409	0.578
mplete:	D%(1980) = 14 + 0.64D%(1978) - 0.27sdiw* - 0.39sdw - 0.66sdl + 30sdem.	123	20	22,311	0.727

nificant at p = 0.05 level; otherwise significant at the p = 0.01 level.

Table A.11 Massachusetts Equations, 1980-1982

Equation		F	t-stat	ESS	R-squa
Registration					
Simple:	D%(1982) = 0 + 0.98D%(1980).	4,924		4,378	0.
Congress					
All towns:					
Simple:	D%(1982) = -10 + 1.23D%(1980).	616		1,126,205	0.
Complete:	D%(1982) = 0 + 0.61D%(1980) - 0.11cdiw - 0.61criw - 0.61cdr - 0.16crd - 0.35collr - 0.19colld* + 37cincd.	622	47	19,739	0.
Contested towns (N = 242):					
Simple:	D%(1982) = 35 + 0.55D%(1980).	176		22,133	0.
Complete:	D%(1982) = 37 + 0.59D%(1980) - 0.09cdiw - 0.15crd* - 0.31collr.	44	6.3	19,770	0.
Senate					
All towns:					
Simple:	D%(1982) = 10 + 0.76D%(1980).	715		60,987	0.
Complete:	D%(1982) = 0 - 0.84D%(1980) + 0.93sdiw + 1.67sriw + 2.54srw + 113sdem - 84sincd.	143	37	26,925	0.
Contested towns (N = 298):					
Simple:	D%(1982) = 13 + 0.74D%(1980).	466		35,167	0.
Complete:	D%(1982) = 11 - 0.85D%(1980) + 1.33sdiw + 1.48sriw + 2.15srw + 106sdem - 84sincd.	143	21	22,906	0.
Governor					
Simple:	D%(1982) = 44 + 0.18D%(1980).	28		21,193	0.
Congress:	D%(1982) = 48 + 0.27D%(1980) - 0.13crd* + 0.35colld - 7.5cincd.*	7	3.4	19,681	0.
Senate:	D%(1982) = 48 + 0.38D%(1980) - 0.31sriw* - 16sdem + 15sincd.	9	5.0	19,602	0.

*significant at p = 0.05 level; otherwise significant at the p = 0.01 level.

Table A.12 Massachusetts Equations, 1982-1984

uation		F	t-stat	ESS	R-square
gistration					
mple:	D%(1984) = 4 + 0.92D%(1982).	4,255		5,024	0.927
ngress					
towns:					
mple:	D%(1984) = 27 + 0.50D%(1982).	633		42,531	0.655
mplete:	D%(1984) = 26 + 0.33D%(1982) + 14cincd.	420	60	34,933	0.716
ntested towns (N = 242):					
mple:	D%(1984) = 45 + 0.22D%(1982).	16		28,043	0.064
mplete:	D%(1984) = 27 + 0.31D%(1982) + 14cincd.	31	37	23,651	0.210
nate					
towns:					
mple:	D%(1984) = 18 + 0.73D%(1982).	275		88,037	0.452
mplete:	D%(1984) = 29 + 0.25D%(1982) - 0.17sriw + 0.21sdw + 20sincd.	156	38	47,777	0.703
ntested towns (N = 303):					
mple:	D%(1984) = 0 + 0.93D%(1982).	462		49,484	0.605
mplete:	D%(1984) = 6* + 0.59D%(1982) -0.30sdiw +0.17sdw +45sincd.	295	43	20,978	0.833

gnificant at p = 0.05 level; otherwise significant at the p = 0.01 level.

Table A.13 Massachusetts Equations, 1984-1986

Equation		F	t-stat	ESS	R-square
Registration					
Simple	D%(1986) = 0 + 0.98D%(1984).	4,061		5,113	0.92
Congress					
All towns (all districts contested):					
Simple	D%(1986) = 0 + 1.07D%(1984)	1,210		41,952	0.78
Complete	D%(1986) = 40 + 0.31D%(1984) +0.26cdiw -0.18criw -27cincr	850	55	13,977	0.92
Senate					
All towns:					
Simple	D%(1986) = -14 + 1.17D%(1984)	686		1,072,532	0.67
Complete	D%(1986) = 0 + 0.45D%(1984) +30sdem	574	158	52,953	0.83
Contested towns (N =254):					
Simple	D%(1986) = 0 + 0.94D%(1984)	434		33,150	0.63
Complete	D%(1986) = 12.5 + 0.50D%(1984) +14sdem* +12cincd*	362	61	16,920	0.81
Governor					
Simple	D%(1986) = 26 + 0.70D%(1984).	309		11,485	0.48
Congress	D%(1986) = 34 + 0.55D%(1984) +0.29cdiw +0.05criw* -17cincd +5cincr.*	126	28	7,613	0.65
Senate	D%(1986) = 30.5 + 0.65D%(1984).	93	---	11,997	0.45

*significant at $p = 0.05$ level; otherwise significant at the $p = 0.01$ level.

Notes

CHAPTER 1: DEFINING THE GERRYMANDER

1. See Bob Benenson, "House of Future at Stake in 1990 Legislative Contests," *Congressional Quarterly Weekly Report* 47 (4 Nov. 1989): 2971.

2. Peter Bragdon, "Incumbents Angling for Edge in 1990's Line Drawing," *Congressional Quarterly Weekly Report* 47 (14 Oct. 1989): 2734.

3. James A. Barnes, "Drawing the Lines," *National Journal* 21 (1 Apr. 1989): 791.

4. See Elmer Griffith, *The Rise and Development of the Gerrymander* (Chicago: Scott Foresman, 1907), 17. The term *gerrymander* appeared in the *Boston Gazette*, 26 Mar. 1812.

5. See Leroy Hardy, "Considering the Gerrymander," *Pepperdine Law Review* 4 (1977): 245, n. 12; see also Griffith, *Rise and Development of the Gerrymander,* 73–74.

6. See, e.g., *Gomillion v. Lightfoot.* This is not to suggest that the Supreme Court should regard or has regarded the rights of political parties and minority groups in the same light. However, the Court's approach to claims of discrimination and gerrymandering by such groups has been predicated on the analysis that the groups can be regarded as similar in their behavior, cohesiveness, etc.

7. Robert Dixon, *Democratic Representation: Reapportionment in Law and Politics* (New York: Oxford, 1968), 460.

8. *Karcher v. Daggett,* 786, Powell, J., dissenting, quoting from *Kirkpatrick v. Preisler,* 538, Fortas, J., concurring.

9. As an example of such cooperative or "bipartisan" gerrymandering, see *Gaffney v. Cummings.* In this case, the Supreme Court permitted a substantial deviation in the populations in Connecticut's state legislative districts because it agreed that Connecticut had a "legitimate state interest" in seeking to ensure the approximately proportional representation of the two major parties. See also *Wright v. Rockefeller,* in which the Court rejected claims that a congressional district that had been drawn to ensure the election of a black candidate was discriminatory.

10. Cf. *Mobile v. Bolden.*

11. Problems of racial gerrymandering are and have been special cases throughout the Court's involvement in the redistricting process, because of the long history of discrimination against blacks. It serves a special purpose in this analysis insofar as it presents a situation in which a gerrymandering claim can be assessed easily due to the durability of race and the ease with which it can be employed as a means of classifying groups of voters.

12. Consider, for example, the rise and disappearance of groups such as the Populists, Hoovercrats, Dixiecrats, and the American Independent party.

13. See, e.g., Justice White's discussion in *Whitcomb v. Chavis.*

14. In *United Jewish Organizations of Williamsburg v. Carey,* the Court disregarded the claims of a Hasidic community that had been divided in the preceding redistricting. The Court's argument, which focused strictly on balancing black and white representation, overlooked the fact that whites were not a homogeneous group. Since the Hasidics were not black, they were regarded as whites and, therefore, in the Court's eyes, had no grounds for challenging the redistricting plan.

15. See, e.g., Richard Hofstadter, *The Idea of a Party System* (Berkeley and Los Angeles: University of California Press, 1969).

16. See, e.g., Sanford Levinson, "Gerrymandering and the Brooding Omnipresence of Proportional Representation: Why It Won't Go Away," *UCLA Law Review* 33 (Oct. 1985): 257.

17. Some systems, for example the two-stage majority system, may tend to disadvantage parties that occupy the extremes of the political spectrum. However, this discrimination is positionally, not ideologically, grounded.

18. See *Baker v. Carr* and *Reynolds v. Sims.*

19. See, e.g., Abigail Thernstrom, *Whose Votes Count?* (Cambridge: Harvard University Press, 1987), 194.

CHAPTER 2: THE COURT'S APPROACH TO GERRYMANDERING
AND REPRESENTATION

1. See, e.g., Section 13 of the Judiciary Act of 1789, 1 stat. 73. See also Laurence Tribe, *American Constitutional Law,* 2d ed. (Mineola, N.Y.: Foundation Press, 1988), 73.

2. See Donald Horowitz, *The Courts and Social Policy* (Washington: Brookings, 1977).

3. Tony Stewart and Sidney Duncombe, "Gerrymandering in the Courts: Threshold of a Second Reapportionment Revolution?" *National Civic Review* 75 (Mar.-Apr. 1987): 88.

4. See *Baker v. Carr;* see also Gordon Baker, *The Reapportionment Revolution* (New York: Random House, 1966).

5. See, e.g., Justice Frankfurter's dissent in *Colegrove v. Green.*

6. See, e.g., the discussion of *Colegrove v. Green,* infra.

7. See also the Court's decision in *Luther v. Borden,* where the Court held that guaranty clause disputes are not justiciable.

8. See Howard Ball, *The Warren Court's Conception of Democracy* (Cranberry, N.J.: Associated University Presses of America, 1971), 84, citing Glendon Schubert, *Judicial Policymaking* (Chicago: Scott Foresman, 1965), 150.

9. See also *Mahan v. Howell, Gaffney v. Cummings,* and *Brown v. Thomson,*

10. See *Karcher v. Daggett.*

11. See, e.g., *Smith v. Allwright,* in which the Court held that white primaries were unconstitutional.

12. See *United States v. Carolene Products Co.,* 152–53, n. 4. See also John Hart Ely, *Democracy and Distrust* (Cambridge: Harvard University Press, 1980), 78.

13. This was the argument set forth by the plaintiffs in *Gomillion v. Lightfoot.*

14. Dixon, *Democratic Representation,* 583.

15. For discussions of the Court's capacity to resolve policy disputes in other areas see, e.g., Horowitz, *Courts and Social Policy;* and Gerald Rosenberg, *The Hollow Hope* (Chicago: University of Chicago Press, 1991).

16. See Schubert, *Judicial Policymaking,* 149–50.

17. See *United States v. Carolene Products Co.* and Ely, *Democracy and Distrust.*

18. *Gomillion,* 553 (stating in dictum that even if the Court could ignore the presence of the nonjusticiable political question and declare the existing electoral system invalid, the state still could chose not to redistrict and force the election of members of the House of Representatives on a statewide ticket).

19. Cf. *Gomillion,* 347 (stating that the state legislature's action in redrawing the city limits did not merely inconvenience petitioners but also "deprived the petitioners of the *municipal franchise and consequent rights*" [emphasis added]).

20. In fact, blacks comprised a majority of the citizenry but a minority of the registered voters. At the time of the redrawing of the map, there were 5,397 black and 1,310 white residents; whites, however, accounted for 600 of the 1,000 registered voters. See Jo Desha Lucas, "Dragon in the Thicket: A Perusal of *Gomillion v. Lightfoot,*" *Supreme Court Review* (1961): 194.

21. See, e.g., *Karcher v. Daggett,* 748–49, Stevens, J., concurring.

22. *Gomillion,* 346, citing *Colegrove,* 549; *Baker,* 249–50, Douglas, J., concurring (broadly concluding without discussion of the difference between *Colegrove* and *Gomillion* that the majority's treatment of *Colegrove* and other cases "removes the only impediment to judicial cognizance of the claims stated in the present complaint"); *Gomillion,* 346.

23. As we shall see, only the groups recognized by the Court are entitled to representation. Thus, the group's definition is a function of judicial opinion, not the activity of group members. See, e.g., the Court's equation of Hasidics with the white majority in *United Jewish Organizations of Williamsburg.*

24. Robert Dixon, "The Warren Court Crusade for the Holy Grail of One-Man, One-Vote," *Supreme Court Review* (1969): 227.

25. Justice Brennan sought to justify the departure from *Colegrove* by noting that the justices had been divided in that decision. Although this acknowledges disagreement on the Court, it explains neither why the *Colegrove* decision stood nor why *Baker* overruled it.

26. See the distinction made in Dixon, *Democratic Representation,* 171. Cf. Dean Alfange, "Gerrymandering and the Constitution: Into the Thorns of the Thicket at Last," *Supreme Court Review* (1986): 175, who perceives only one line of cases.

27. See, e.g., *Kirkpatrick v. Preisler* (prohibiting even slight deviations from strict population equality in congressional districts unless justifiable) and *Karcher v. Daggett* (requiring near absolute population equality).

28. See also Pamela Karlan, "Maps and Misreadings: The Role of Geographic Compactness in Racial Vote Dilution Litigation," *Harvard Civil Rights–Civil Liberties Law Review* 24 (Winter 1989): 173.

29. For example, the Court ruled in *Gaffney v. Cummings* that a state's attempt to achieve proportional representation of the major parties in the legislature was such an objective. In *United Jewish Organizations of Williamsburg v. Carey,* New York's at-

tempt to maximize black representation justified the division of a Hasidic community in Brooklyn.

30. Justice O'Connor's concurrence, *Davis*, 148–50; Justice White's opinion, *Davis*, 122–24 (stating that the issue "is not that anyone is deprived of a vote or that any person's vote is not counted. Rather, it is that one . . . [elector] may vote for and his district be represented by only one legislator, while his neighbor in the adjoining district votes for and is represented by two or more" [123]).

31. Dixon, "Warren Court Crusade," 228.

32. Group cohesion cannot be assumed. As shown in chapter 6, below, variability in the size and partisan behavior of voting blocs suggests that partisanship is not a cohesive bond.

33. Dixon, *Democratic Representation*, 269.

34. Dixon, "Warren Court Crusade," 229.

35. See, e.g., *White v. Regester*, holding that the disestablishment of multimember districts is warranted in light of the discrimination against blacks and Mexican-Americans; see *Whitcomb*, 124.

36. Dixon, "Warren Court Crusade," 227.

37. Dixon, *Democratic Representation*, 437–38.

38. See, e.g., Linda Lichter, "Who Speaks for Black America?" *Public Opinion* 8 (Aug.-Sept. 1958): 41.

39. Dixon, "Warren Court Crusade," 244.

40. *Kirkpatrick*, 531 (holding that states must create congressional districts which provide equal representation for equal numbers of people with only a slight margin of error for "unavoidable" variances).

41. Despite the fact that both *Gaffney* and *Karcher* involved obvious gerrymanders, the Court approached them differently. Whereas the Court regarded *Gaffney* as a case of "benign" gerrymandering (as a result of the legitimacy of the state's interest in balancing party strength in its legislature), it chose to treat *Karcher*—an obvious gerrymander—as an equal protection case. See Alfange, "Gerrymandering and the Constitution," 210. See also Larry Light, "New Jersey Map Imaginative Gerrymander," *Congressional Quarterly Weekly Report* 40 (22 May 1982): 1190.

42. *Karcher*, 761, n. 28, citing Tribe, *American Constitutional Law*, 756.

43. Dixon, *Democratic Representation*, 269.

44. Dixon, *Democratic Representation*, 437–38.

45. Consider, for example, the defeat of Margaret Heckler by Barney Frank in the 1982 Massachusetts congressional race. Frank and Heckler had been forced to run against each other because Massachusetts had lost a seat as a result of the new census. Frank beat Heckler in a district that had been redrawn largely from Heckler's old district. See *State Politics and Redistricting*, pt. 1 (Washington, D.C.: Congressional Quarterly Press, 1982), 20.

CHAPTER 3: THE POLITICAL SCIENCE MODEL OF VOTING BEHAVIOR AND ITS IMPORTANCE FOR REDISTRICTING ANALYSIS

1. See, e.g., Howard R. Swearer, "The Functions of Soviet Local Elections," *Midwest Journal of Political Science* 5 (May 1961): 129.

2. Angus Campbell et al., *The American Voter* (Chicago: Midway Reprints, 1980).

3. See Randall Calvert and John Ferejohn, "Coattail Voting in Recent Presidential Elections," *American Political Science Review* 77 (June 1983): 407; and John Ferejohn and Randall Calvert, "Presidential Coattails in Historical Perspective," *American Journal of Political Science* 28 (Feb. 1984): 127.

4. V. O. Key, "A Theory of Critical Elections," *Journal of Politics* 17 (Feb. 1955): 3.

5. Campbell et al., *American Voter*, 135.

6. Key, "Critical Elections," 3–4.

7. V. O. Key, "Secular Realignment and the Party System," *Journal of Politics* 21 (May 1959): 198–99.

8. Key, "Secular Realignment," 203.

9. Warren Miller, "The Cross-National Use of Party Identification as a Stimulus to Political Inquiry," in *Party Identification and Beyond,* ed. Ian Budge, Ivor Crewe, and Dennis Farlie (New York: Wiley, 1976), 22.

10. Philip Converse, "Of Time and Partisan Stability," *Comparative Political Studies* 2 (July 1969): 139.

11. Campbell et al., *American Voter*, 121.

12. Philip Converse, "The Concept of a Normal Vote," in *Elections and the Political Order,* ed. Angus Campbell (New York: Wiley, 1966), 14.

13. Campbell et al., *American Voter*, 531.

14. In 1967, Gerald Pomper added a fourth category, "converting" elections, in which "the majority party retains its position, but there is a considerable change in its voter base." See Gerald Pomper, "Classification of Presidential Elections," *Journal of Politics* 29 (Aug. 1967): 535.

15. Philip Converse, "The Nature of Belief Systems in Mass Publics," in *Ideology and Discontent,* ed. David Apter (New York: Free Press, 1964), 231.

16. Miller, "Cross-National Use of Party Identification," 24.

17. Converse, "Belief Systems," 231.

18. V. O. Key, *The Responsible Electorate* (Cambridge: Balknap Press of Harvard University, 1966).

19. Philip Converse, book review of *The Responsible Electorate, Political Science Quarterly* 81 (Dec. 1966): 632 (emphasis in original).

20. Walter Dean Burnham, "Theory and Voting Research," *American Political Science Review* 68 (Sept. 1974): 1002.

21. Walter Dean Burnham, "Those High Nineteenth-Century American Voting Turnouts: Fact or Fiction?" *Journal of Interdisciplinary History* 16 (Spring 1986): 613.

22. Walter Dean Burnham, "The System of 1896: An Analysis," in *The Evolution of American Electoral Systems,* ed. Paul Kleppner (Westport, Conn.: Greenwood Press, 1981), 147.

23. Walter Dean Burnham, "Rejoinder to Comments," *American Political Science Review* 68 (Sept. 1974): 1051.

24. Burnham, "Theory and Voting Research," 1019.

25. Burnham, "Rejoinder to Comments," 1057; Richard Nie, Sidney Verba, and John Petrocik, *The Changing American Voter,* (Cambridge: Harvard University Press, 1979).

26. Burnham, "System of 1896," 157.

27. Walter Dean Burnham, "The Politics of Crisis," *Journal of Interdisciplinary History* 8 (Spring 1978): 759 (emphasis in original). See also Ronald Inglehart, "The Silent Revolution in Europe: Intergenerational Change in Post-Industrial Societies," *American Political Science Review* 65 (Dec. 1971): 991; Ronald Inglehart, "Post-Materialism in an Environment of Security," *American Political Science Review* 75 (Dec. 1981): 880; and Ronald Inglehart, "The Changing Structure of Political Cleavages in Western Democracies," in *Electoral Change in Advanced Industrial Democracies,* ed. Russell Dalton, Scott C. Flanagan, and Paul Allen Beck (Princeton: Princeton University Press, 1981). See also, e.g., C. Everett Ladd and Charles Hadley, *Transformations of the American Party System* (New York: Norton, 1978).

28. Burnham, "Politics of Crisis," 762.

29. See *Davis v. Bandemer.*

30. See, e.g., Barbara Hinckley, *Congressional Elections* (Washington: Congressional Quarterly Press, 1981); and Gary Jacobson, *The Politics of Congressional Elections* (Boston: Little, Brown, 1983).

31. See generally Gerald Sullivan and Michael Kenney, *The Race for the Eighth* (New York: Harper and Row, 1987).

CHAPTER 4: THEORIES AND METHODS OF GERRYMANDERING ANALYSIS

1. Two exemplary statements to this effect can be found in Graham Gudgin and P. J. Taylor, *Seats, Votes, and the Spatial Organization of Elections* (London: Pion, 1979), 36; and Stephen E. Gottlieb, "Fashioning a Test for Gerrymandering," *Journal of Legislation* 15 (1988): 1.

2. See, e.g., Gottlieb, "Test for Gerrymandering," 9.

3. See generally *Political Gerrymandering and the Courts* ed. Bernard Grofman (New York: Agathon, 1990); and Bernard Grofman, "Criteria for Districting: A Social Science Perspective," *UCLA Law Review* 33 (Oct. 1985): 77.

4. See generally Gudgin and Taylor, *Seats, Votes.*

5. See Grofman, "Criteria for Districting," 131–49.

6. See discussion of the effects of collapsed districts on representation in Bernard Grofman, "Excerpts from First Declaration in *Badham v. Eu,*" *Political Science and Politics* 18 (Summer 1985): 547–48.

7. See Hinckley, *Congressional Elections;* and Jacobson, *Politics of Congressional Elections.*

8. See, e.g., Charles Backstrom, Leonard Robins, and Scott Eller, "Issues in Gerrymandering: An Exploratory Measure of Partisan Gerrymandering Applied to Minnesota," *Minnesota Law Review* 62 (July 1978): 1121; and Richard Niemi, "The Relationship Between Seats and Votes: The Ultimate Question in Political Gerrymandering," *UCLA Law Review* 33 (Oct. 1985): 185, respectively. See also Gudgin and Taylor, *Seats, Votes,* and Rein Taagpera and Matthew Shugart, *Seats and Votes* (New Haven: Yale University Press, 1989).

9. Backstrom et al., "Issues in Gerrymandering," 1131.

10. Ibid., 1132–33, citing William Flanigan and Nancy Zingale, *Political Behavior of the American Electorate,* 3d ed. (Dubuque, Iowa: W. C. Brown, 1975), 44.

11. For a discussion of ballot fatigue and roll-off see, e.g., Jack L. Walker, "Ballot Forms and Voter Fatigue: An Analysis of the Office Block and Party Column Ballots," *Midwest Journal of Political Science* 10 (Nov. 1966): 448.

12. See, e.g., David Butler and Stephen Van Beck, "Why Not Swing?" *PS: Political Science and Politics* 23 (June 1990): 178; see also Niemi, "Relationship Between Seats and Votes"; Niemi, "The Swing Ratio as a Measure of Partisan Gerrymandering," in *Political Gerrymandering and the Courts,* ed. Grofman, 171; and Richard Niemi and John Deegan, "A Theory of Political Redistricting," *American Political Science Review* 72 (Dec. 1978): 1304.

13. See especially Niemi and Deegan, "Theory of Political Redistricting," 1306.

14. See, e.g., Gary King, "Representation through Legislative Redistricting: A Stochastic Approach," *American Journal of Political Science* 33 (Nov. 1989): 787; and Gary King and Robert Browning, "Democratic Representation and Partisan Bias in Congressional Elections," *American Political Science Review* 81 (Dec. 1987): 1251.

15. Data are drawn from *Massachusetts Elections Statistics,* Public Document 43 (Boston: Office of the Secretary of the Commonwealth), and *Statement of Vote* (Hartford: Office of the Secretary of State).

CHAPTER 5: THE STATES AS POLITICAL UNITS

1. See Samuel Kernell and Bernard Grofman, "Determining the Predictability of Partisan Voting Patterns in California Elections, 1978–1984," in *Political Gerrymandering and the Courts,* ed. Grofman

2. Connecticut's Democratic party organization, established and consolidated by John M. Bailey, has dominated the state's politics since the 1950s. See e.g., Joseph Lieberman, *The Power Broker: A Biography of John M. Bailey, Modern Political Boss* (Boston: Houghton Mifflin, 1966); and Neal R. Peirce, *The New England States* (New York: Norton, 1972), 190–200. For the dominance of the Democratic party in Massachusetts politics, see, generally, John Kenneth White, *The Fractured Electorate* (Hanover, N.H.: University Press of New England, 1983).

3. This is not to say that incumbents are invulnerable. Massachusetts is known for its bloody Democratic primary battles and incessant factional feuding within the party itself. As a result, primary challenges are usually more ominous threats to an incumbent's survival than any general election. See, generally, White, *Fractured Electorate;* and Sullivan and Kenney, *Race for the Eighth.*

4. Comparable data for Connecticut were not provided.

5. Due to the significant number of uncontested elections, I do not include towns from districts where Democrats failed to run a candidate.

6. In fact, the Republican rate of participation *did* remain quite high in both 1988 and 1990. In state senate elections, 47 percent of the vote in both years was cast for Republican candidates. At the congressional level, 50.1 percent and 52.6 percent of the vote were cast for Republican candidates in 1988 and 1990, respectively.

7. See White, *Fractured Electorate,* 58–64.

CHAPTER 6: THE IMPACT OF REDISTRICTING AND INCUMBENCY ON
VOTING BEHAVIOR

1. See appendix A for a discussion of the categories and my use of dummy variables.

2. See, e.g., Alan Agresti and Barbara Finlay, *Statistical Methods for the Social Sciences,* 2d ed. (San Francisco: Dellen MacMillan, 1986).

3. From this point onward, I refer to the prediction equations for contested districts only, unless otherwise noted.

4. The complete equations describe only the behavior of towns in districts held by the Democratic party. Since Silvio Conte, the lone Republican incumbent, was unopposed, his towns are not included in the prediction equation for these two years.

5. See *State Politics and Redistricting,* pt. 1 (Washington: Congressional Quarterly Press, 1982), 20.

6. Bragdon, "Incumbents Angling for Edge," 2735.

CHAPTER 7: CONCLUSION: POLITICAL SCIENCE, REPRESENTATION,
AND POLITICS

1. Key, "Secular Realignment," 203.

2. Burnham, "System of 1896."

3. Key, "Critical Elections."

4. See, e.g., Howard Scarrow, "Partisan Gerrymandering: Invidious or Benevolent?" *Journal of Politics* 44 (Aug. 1982): 810.

5. See, e.g., Levinson, "Gerrymandering and the Brooding Omnipresence of Proportional Representation."

6. See Leon Epstein, *Political Parties in Western Democracies* (New Brunswick, N.J.: Transaction Books, 1980), 201.

7. See, e.g., the extensive discussion of the merits of divers electoral systems in J. Paul Johnston and Harvey Pasis, *Representation and Electoral Systems: A Canadian Perspective* (Scarborough: Prentice Hall Canada, 1990); Bernard Grofman and Arend Lijphart, *Electoral Laws and Their Political Consequences* (New York: Agathon, 1986); Arend Lijphart and Bernard Grofman, *Choosing An Electoral System* (New York: Praeger, 1984); and Andrew M. Carstairs, *A Short History of Electoral Systems in Western Europe* (London: George Allen and Unwin, 1980).

8. A thorough discussion of the visions of constituencies is presented in Nancy Maveety, *Representation Rights and the Burger Years* (Ann Arbor: University of Michigan Press, 1991).

9. See, e.g., "Political Pornography—II," *Wall Street Journal,* 4 Feb. 1992; and "No Grey Areas," *Economist,* 8 Feb. 1992, 26, both discussing the contortions built into the North Carolina congressional district map.

10. See, e.g., Pamela Karlan, "Maps and Misreadings: The Role of Geographic Compactness in Racial Vote Dilution Litigation," *Harvard Civil Rights–Civil Liberties Law Review* 24 (Winter 1989): 173; and Edward Still, "Alternatives to Single-Member Districts," in *Minority Vote Dilution,* ed. Chandler Davidson (Washington: Howard University Press, 1989).

11. See *Badham v. Eu.*

12. On the legislative process, see, e.g., *Luther v. Borden, Coleman v. Miller,* and *Powell v. McCormick.* On party organization, see, e.g., *Smith v. Allwright,* where the Court declared white primaries unconstitutional; *Rosario v. Rockefeller,* where the Court sustained New York's thirty-day enrollment requirement as a prerequisite for voting in a primary; and *Tashjian v. Connecticut,* where the Court struck down a law requiring that participants in a party's primary register with that same party.

13. See, e.g., *Luther v. Borden* and *Coleman v. Miller.*

14. Horowitz, *Courts and Social Policy.*

15. Alexander Bickel, *The Supreme Court and the Idea of Progress* (New Haven: Yale University Press, 1978), 87.

16. Hannah Pitkin, *The Concept of Representation* (Berkeley and Los Angeles: University of California Press, 1967), 145.

17. In a concurring opinion in *Jacobellis v. Ohio,* 378 US 184 (1964), Justice Stewart exposed his unscientific approach to identifying pornography: "I know it when I see it."

18. James Ceaser, *Liberal Democracy and Political Science* (Baltimore: Johns Hopkins University Press, 1990), 37.

Bibliography

Agresti, Alan, and Barbara Finlay. *Statistical Methods for the Social Sciences.* 2d ed. San Francisco: Dellen MacMillan, 1986.

Alfange, Dean. "Gerrymandering and the Constitution: Into the Thorns of the Thicket at Last." *Supreme Court Review* (1986): 175–257.

Apter, David. *Ideology and Discontent.* New York: Free Press, 1964.

Backstrom, Charles, Leonard Robins, and Scott Eller, "Issues in Gerrymandering: An Exploratory Measure of Partisan Gerrymandering Applied to Minnesota." *Minnesota Law Review* 62 (July 1978): 1121–57.

Baker, Gordon. *The Reapportionment Revolution.* New York: Random House, 1966.

Ball, Howard. *The Warren Court's Conception of Democracy.* Cranberry, N.J.: Associated University Presses of America, 1971.

Barnes, James. "Drawing the Lines." *National Journal* 21 (1 Apr. 1989): 787–91.

Basehart, Harry. "The Seats/Votes Relationship and the Identification of Partisan Gerrymandering in State Legislatures." *American Politics Quarterly* 15 (Oct. 1987): 484–97.

Benenson, Bob. "House of Future at Stake in 1990 Legislative Contests." *Congressional Quarterly* 47 (4 Nov. 1989): 2971–3004.

Bickel, Alexander. *The Least Dangerous Branch.* Indianapolis: Bobbs-Merrill, 1980.

———. *The Supreme Court and the Idea of Progress.* New Haven: Yale University Press, 1978.

Bragdon, Peter. "Incumbents Angling for Edge in 1990's Line-Drawing." *Congressional Quarterly* 47 (14 Oct. 1989): 2734–38.

Budge, Ian, Ivor Crewe, and Dennis Fairlie, eds. *Party Identification and Beyond.* New York: Wiley, 1976.

Burnham, Walter Dean. "Those High Nineteenth-Century American Voting Turnouts: Fact or Fiction?" *Journal of Interdisciplinary History* 16 (Spring 1986): 613–44.

———. "The Politics of Crisis." *Journal of Interdisciplinary History* 8 (Spring 1978): 747–63.

———. "Rejoinder to Comments." *American Political Science Review* 68 (Sept. 1974): 1050–57.

———. "The System of 1896: An Analysis." In *The Evolution of American Electoral Systems,* ed. Paul Kleppner. Westport, Conn.: Greenwood Press, 1981.

———. "Theory and Voting Research." *American Political Science Review* 68 (Sept. 1974): 1002–23.

Butler, David, and Stephen Van Beck. "Why Not Swing?" *PS: Political Science and Politics* 23 (June 1990): 178–84.

Cain, Bruce. *The Reapportionment Puzzle.* Berkeley and Los Angeles: University of California Press, 1983.

Calvert, Randall, and John Ferejohn. "Coattail Voting in Recent Presidential Elections." *American Political Science Review* 77 (June 1983): 407–18.

Campbell, Angus, ed. *Elections and the Political Order.* New York: Wiley, 1966.

Campbell, Angus, Philip Converse, Donald Stokes, and Warren Miller, *The American Voter.* Chicago: Midway Reprints, 1980.

Carstairs, Andrew M., *A Short History of Electoral Systems in Western Europe.* London: George Allen and Unwin, 1980.

Ceaser, James. *Liberal Democracy and Political Science.* Baltimore: Johns Hopkins University Press, 1990.

Clubb, Jerome, and Howard Allen. *Electoral Change and Stability in American Political History.* New York: Free Press, 1971.

Converse, Philip. "The Concept of a Normal Vote." In *Elections and the Political Order,* ed. Angus Campbell. New York: Wiley, 1966.

————. "The Nature of Belief Systems in Mass Publics." In *Ideology and Discontent,* ed. David Apter. New York: Free Press, 1964.

————. "Of Time and Partisan Stability." *Comparative Political Studies* 2 (July 1969): 139–71.

————. Book review of *The Responsible Electorate. Political Science Quarterly* 81 (Dec. 1966): 629–33.

Cranor, John, Gary L. Grawley, and Raymond H. Scheele. "The Anatomy of a Gerrymander." *American Journal of Political Science* 33 (Feb. 1989): 222–39.

Dalton, Russell J., Scott C. Flanagan, and Paul Alan Beck, eds. *Electoral Change in Advanced Industrial Democracies.* Princeton: Princeton University Press, 1981.

Davidson, Chandler, ed. *Minority Vote Dilution.* Washington: Howard University Press, 1989.

Dixon, Robert. *Democratic Representation: Reapportionment in Law and Politics.* New York: Oxford University Press, 1968.

————. "The Warren Court Crusade for the Holy Grail of One-Man, One-Vote." *Supreme Court Review* (1969): 219–64.

Ely, John Hart. *Democracy and Distrust.* Cambridge: Harvard University Press, 1980.

Epstein, Leon. *Political Parties in Western Democracies.* New Brunswick, N.J.: Transaction Books, 1980.

Ferejohn, John, and Randall Calvert. "Presidential Coattails in Historical Perspective." *American Journal of Political Science* 28 (Feb. 1984): 126–46.

Fiorina, Morris. *Retrospective Voting in American National Elections.* New Haven: Yale University Press, 1981.

Flanigan, William, and Nancy Zingale. *Political Behavior of the American Electorate.* 3d ed. Dubuque, Iowa: W. C. Brown, 1975.

Gelman, Andrew, and Gary King. "Estimating Incumbency Advantage without Bias." *American Journal of Political Science* 34 (Nov. 1990): 1142–64.

Gottlieb, Stephen E. "Fashioning a Test for Gerrymandering." *Journal of Legislation* 15 (1988): 1–14.

Griffith, Elmer. *The Rise and Development of the Gerrymander.* Chicago: Scott Foresman, 1907.

Grofman, Bernard. "Criteria for Districting: A Social Science Perspective." *UCLA Law Review* 33 (Oct. 1985): 77–185.

————. "Excerpts from First Declaration in *Badham v. Eu.*" *PS: Political Science and Politics* 18 (Summer 1985): 547–48.

Grofman, B., ed. *Political Gerrymandering and the Courts.* New York: Agathon, 1990.

_____. "Symposium: Political Science Goes to Court." *PS: Political Science and Politics* 18 (Summer 1985): 538–82.

Grofman, Bernard, and Arend Lijphart. *Electoral Laws and Their Political Conse-quences.* New York: Agathon, 1986.

Gudgin, Graham, and P. J. Taylor. *Seats, Votes and the Spatial Organization of Elec-tions.* London: Pion, 1979.

Hardy, Leroy, "Considering the Gerrymander." *Pepperdine Law Review* 4 (1977): 243–84.

Hinckley, Barbara. *Congressional Elections.* Washington: Congressional Quarterly Press, 1981.

Hofstadter, Richard. *The Idea of a Party System.* Berkeley and Los Angeles: University of California Press, 1969.

Horowitz, Donald. *The Courts and Social Policy.* Washington: Brookings, 1977.

Inglehart, Ronald. "The Changing Structure of Political Cleavages in Western Democra-cies." In *Electoral Change in Advanced Industrial Democracies,* ed. Russell Dalton, Scott C. Flanagan, and Paul Allen Beck. Princeton: Princeton University Press, 1981.

_____. "Post-Materialism in an Environment of Security." *American Political Science Review* 75 (Dec. 1981): 880–901.

_____. "The Silent Revolution in Europe: Intergenerational Change in Post-Industrial Societies." *American Political Science Review* 65 (Dec. 1971): 991–1017.

Jacobson, Gary. *The Politics of Congressional Elections.* Boston: Little, Brown, 1983.

Johnson, Charles A., and Bradley Canon. *Judicial Policies: Implementation and Im-pact.* Washington: Congressional Quarterly, 1984.

Johnston, J. Paul, and Harvey Pasis. *Representation and Electoral Systems: A Canadian Perspective.* Scarborough, Ontario: Prentice Hall, Canada, 1990.

Karlan, Pamela. "Maps and Misreadings: The Role of Geographic Compactness in Racial Vote Dilution Litigation." *Harvard Civil Rights–Civil Liberties Law Review* 24 (Winter 1989): 173–248.

Kernell, Samuel, and Bernard Grofman. "Determining the Predictability of Partisan Voting Patterns in California Elections, 1978–1984." In *Political Gerrymandering and the Courts,* ed. Bernard Grofman, New York: Agathon, 1990.

Key, V. O. *The Responsible Electorate.* Cambridge: Belknap Press of Harvard Univer-sity, 1966.

_____. "Secular Realignment and the Party System." *Journal of Politics* 21 (May 1959): 198–210.

_____. *Southern Politics.* Reprint. Knoxville: University of Tennessee Press, 1984.

_____. "A Theory of Critical Elections." *Journal of Politics* 17 (Feb. 1955): 3–18.

King, Gary. "Representation through Legislative Redistricting: A Stochastic Ap-proach." *American Journal of Political Science* 33 (Nov. 1989): 787–824.

King, Gary, and Robert Browning. "Democratic Representation and Partisan Bias in Congressional Elections." *American Political Science Review* 81 (Dec. 1987): 1251–73.

Kleppner, Paul. *The Evolution of American Electoral Systems.* Westport, Conn.: Green-wood Press, 1981.

Ladd, C. Everett, and Charles Hadley. *Transformations of the American Party System.* New York: Norton, 1978.

Levinson, Sanford. "Gerrymandering and the Brooding Omnipresence of Proportional Representation: Why It Won't Go Away." *UCLA Law Review* 33 (Oct. 1985): 257–82.

Lichter, Linda. "Who Speaks for Black America?" *Public Opinion* 8 (Aug.-Sept. 1985): 41–47.

Lieberman, Joseph. *The Power Broker: A Biography of John M. Bailey, Modern Political Boss*. Boston: Houghton Mifflin, 1966.

Lijphart, Arend, and Bernard Grofman. *Choosing an Electoral System*. New York: Praeger, 1984.

Light, Larry. "New Jersey Map Imaginative Gerrymander." *Congressional Quarterly* 40 (22 May 1982): 1190–99.

Lucas, Jo Desha. "Dragon in the Thicket: A Perusal of *Gomillion v. Lightfoot*." *Supreme Court Review* (1961): 194–244.

Maveety, Nancy. *Representation Rights and the Burger Years*. Ann Arbor: University of Michigan Press, 1991.

Miller, Warren. "The Cross-National Use of Party Identification as a Stimulus to Political Inquiry." In *Party Identification and Beyond*, ed. Ian Budge, Ivor Crewe, and Dennis Farlie. New York: Wiley, 1976.

Neter, John, William Wasserman, and Michael Kutner. *Applied Linear Regression Models*. 2d ed. Chicago: Richard D. Irwin, 1989.

Nie, Richard, Sidney Verba, and John Petrocik. *The Changing American Voter*. Cambridge: Harvard University Press, 1979.

Niemi, Richard. "The Relationship between Seats and Votes: The Ultimate Question in Political Gerrymandering." *UCLA Law Review* 33 (Oct. 1985): 185–212.

————. "The Swing Ratio as a Measure of Partisan Gerrymandering." In *Political Gerrymandering and the Courts*, ed. Bernard Grofman. New York: Agathon, 1990.

Niemi, Richard, and John Deegan. "A Theory of Political Redistricting." *American Political Science Review* 72 (Dec. 1978): 1304–23.

Peirce, Neal R. *The New England States*. New York: Norton, 1972.

Phillips, Kevin. *American Political Report*. 16 Nov. 1984.

————. *American Political Report*. 11 Jan. 1985.

Pomper, Gerald. "Classification of Presidential Elections." *Journal of Politics* 29 (Aug. 1967): 535–66.

Pitikin, Hannah. *The Concept of Representation*. Berkeley and Los Angeles: University of California Press, 1967.

Rosenberg, Gerald. *The Hollow Hope*. Chicago: University of Chicago Press, 1991.

Scarrow, Howard. "Partisan Gerrymandering: Invidious or Benevolent?" *Journal of Politics* 44 (Aug. 1982): 810–21.

Schubert, Glendon. *Judicial Policymaking*. Chicago: Scott Foresman, 1965.

State Politics and Redistricting. Pt. 1. Washington: Congressional Quarterly Press, 1982.

Stewart, Tony, and Sidney Duncombe. "Gerrymandering in the Courts: Threshold of a Second Reapportionment Revolution?" *National Civic Review* 75 (Mar.-Apr. 1987): 88–98.

Still, Edward. "Alternatives to Single-Member Districts." In *Minority Vote Dilution*, ed. Chandler Davidson. Washington: Howard University Press, 1989.

Sullivan, Gerald, and Michael Kenney. *The Race for the Eighth*. New York: Harper and Row, 1987.

Swearer, Howard. "The Functions of Soviet Local Elections." *Midwest Journal of Political Science* 5 (May 1961): 129–50.

Taagpera, Rein, and Matthew Shugart. *Seats and Votes.* New Haven: Yale University Press, 1989.

Thernstrom, Abigail. *Whose Votes Count?* Cambridge: Harvard University Press, 1987.

Tribe, Laurence. *American Constitutional Law.* 2d ed. Mineola, N.Y.: Foundation Press, 1988.

Walker, Jack L. "Ballot Forms and Voter Fatigue: An Analysis of the Office Block and Party Column Ballots." *Midwest Journal of Political Science* 10 (Nov. 1966): 448–63.

White, John Kenneth. *The Fractured Electorate.* Hanover, N.H.: University Press of New England, 1983.

LIST OF CASES

Badham v. Eu, 694 F. Supp. 664 (1988).
Baker v. Carr, 369 US 186 (1962).
Brown v. Thompson, 462 US 835 (1983).
Colegrove v. Green, 328 US 549 (1946).
Coleman v. Miller, 307 US 433 (1939).
Davis v. Bandemer, 478 US 109 (1986).
Fortson v. Dorsey, 379 US 433 (1965).
Gaffney v. Cummings, 412 US 735 (1973).
Gomillion v. Lightfoot, 364 US 339 (1960).
Grey v. Sanders, 372 US 368 (1963).
Karcher v. Daggett, 462 US 725 (1983).
Kirkpatrick v. Preisler, 394 US 526 (1969).
Kirksey v. Board of Supervisors of Hinds County, 554 F.2d 139 (1977).
Luther v. Borden, 48 US (7 How.) 1 (1849).
MacDougal v. Green, 335 US 281 (1948).
Mahan v. Howell, 410 US 315 (1973).
Mobile v. Bolden, 466 US 55 (1980).
Powell v. McCormick, 395 US 486 (1969).
Reynolds v. Sims, 377 US 533 (1964).
Rogers v. Lodge, 463 US 613 (1982).
Smith v. Allwright, 321 US 649 (1944).
Tashjian v. Connecticut, 479 US 208 (1986).
Thornburg v. Gingles, 478 US 30 (1986).
United Jewish Organizations of Williamsburg v. Carey, 430 US 144 (1976).
United States v. Carolene Products Co., 304 US 144 (1938).
Wesberry v. Sanders, 376 US 1 (1964).
Whitcomb v. Chavis, 403 US 124 (1971).
White v. Regester, 412 US 744 (1973).
Wright v. Rockefeller, 376 US 52 (1964).
Rosario v. Rockefeller, 410 US 752 (1973).

Index